History on your Doorstep

Volume 2

Six more stories of Dublin history

by Dublin City Council's Historians in Residence
Maeve Casserly, James Curry, Bernard Kelly, Cormac Moore,
Mary Muldowney & Catherine Scuffil

Edited by Maeve Casserly and Cormac Moore

Dublin City Council 2019
Decade of Commemorations Publications Series

First published 2019 by
Dublin City Council
c/o Dublin City Libraries
138-144 Pearse Street
Dublin 2

www.dublincity.ie

 Comhairle Cathrach
Bhaile Átha Cliath
Dublin City Council

Designed by Source Design
Printed by The Printed Image

ISBN – 978-0-9500512-7-7

Table of Contents

Réamhrá / **Foreword**

Following the success of last year's book *History on Your Doorstep; six stories of Dublin history*, Dublin City Council's historians in residence have researched and written another six stories looking at the history of this great city of Dublin.

Events of 100 years ago have been the inspiration for some of the chapters; Dr. Kathleen Lynn, such an important figure in the Irish revolutionary and suffrage movements, founded the innovative children's hospital St. Ultan's in 1919, the same year that the War of Independence began, which features in another chapter looking at Dublin Corporation at this time of great change and upheaval in the city. Read about the four social housing schemes on the southside of the city built about 100 years ago and there's also a focus on old workplaces of Dublin now gone, like Lemon's sweets, the cattle market or Jacob's biscuit factory.

As a proud Finglas-man, I am especially pleased that there is a chapter on the famous Finglas uilleann piper Séamus Ennis. 2019 is the centenary of the birth of this gifted musician whose musical skills are legendary and have influenced countless others, while the music, songs and stories he collected around the country in the 1940s are the bedrock of Ireland's priceless folklore collection.

Pick up a free copy of this great book in your local library and then, if you want to read deeper, you can borrow history books in your local library, you might especially like the selection of Dublin memoirs the historians have picked out as their favourites.

PAUL MCAULIFFE
Lord Mayor of Dublin

Dublin City Council Historians in Residence Project

A team of six Historians in Residence work across Dublin City to talk to people about history and promote its sources, especially documents, photos and books in Dublin City Libraries and Archives. The Historians in Residence project is part of Dublin City Council's work under the Decade of Commemorations (1912-22) designation and strives to break down barriers to history.

Who are they?

MAEVE CASSERLY has an MPhil in Public History and Cultural Heritage from Trinity College Dublin and is completing her PhD in University College Dublin. Her most recent publication is 'Exhibiting Éire: representations of women in the centenary commemorations of the Easter Rising,' in (ed.) Oona Frawley *Women and the Decade of Centenaries* (2019). Maeve is a 2019/2020 Fulbright-Creative Ireland Fellow. She is the Historian in Residence for the South East area of Dublin City.

JAMES CURRY received his PhD in History and Digital Humanities from NUI Galway in 2017. The author of a book about Dublin cartoonist Ernest Kavanagh plus many articles and co-authored books dealing with modern Irish history, James is a former committee member of the Irish Labour History Society and a founding member of NUI Galway's Irish Centre for the Histories of Labour and Class. James is the Historian in Residence for the North West area of Dublin City.

BERNARD KELLY received his PhD from NUI Galway in 2010 and did his postdoctoral work at the University of Edinburgh. He is the author of two books on Ireland and the Second World War, and is currently Historian in Residence based at Dublin City Library & Archives on Pearse Street.

Cormac Moore has an MA in Modern Irish History from University College Dublin and is completing his PhD at DeMontfort University, Leicester. He is Historian in Residence for Dublin North Central and is author of *Birth of the Border: The Impact of Partition in Ireland* (2019), *The Irish Soccer Split* (2015) and *The GAA V Douglas Hyde: The Removal of Ireland's First President as GAA Patron* (2012).

Mary Muldowney holds a PhD in History from Trinity College Dublin and also a postgraduate qualification in Adult Continuing Education and Training from the National University of Ireland at Maynooth. She is the Historian in Residence for the Dublin Central area and works as an adult education consultant for community groups and trade unions. Mary is one of the organisers of the Stoneybatter & Smithfield People's History Project and a founder and former director of the Oral History Network of Ireland.

Catherine Scuffil has an MA in Local History from Maynooth University. She is currently the Historian in Residence for Dublin South Central which includes the historic Liberties and some of the city's oldest suburbs. Catherine has written a number of local history books and an abridged version of her MA thesis was awarded the Old Dublin Society's silver medal in 2018.

Contact them at commemorations@dublincity.ie, Twitter and Facebook @DubHistorians www.dublincity.ie/decadeofcommemorations.

St. Ultan's: a ground-breaking institution for the health and well-being of women, children and doctors alike

Maeve Casserly, Historian in Residence, Dublin South East

St. Ultan's hospital was founded in May 1919 by Dr. Kathleen Lynn and her partner Madeleine Ffrench-Mullen and was, from its outset, an innovative institution run by women for women and children.

A combination of factors led to the formation of St. Ultan's as the first Irish hospital dedicated to paediatric care, and one of only a few hospitals in Ireland run almost entirely by women. The First World War allowed many women to gain organisational and logistical experience running charity and voluntary aid institutions outside the home. It also gave many women the opportunity to gain skills and confidence in leadership roles. For example, the organisation of hundreds of war supply depots across the country, staffed by thousands of women, was often administered by women too. Following the education and voting reforms of the late 1800s and early 1900s a new generation of highly trained female doctors, like Dr. Kathleen Lynn, were eager to use their skills to make a mark on their field. The environment of St. Ultan's, headed by prominent figures in medicine and women's suffrage, encouraged its staff to be innovators. This included Dr. Dorothy Stopford-Price who played a key role in the fight against childhood tuberculosis in Ireland.

The circumstances of the First World War created the impetus for St. Ultan's, but it was the work of women like Dr. Lynn and Dr. Stopford-Price that turned this hospital into a revolutionary organisation for change in paediatric healthcare in Ireland. St. Ultan's helped female doctors make their mark in the medical world and part of its legacy for professional women was the confidence it inspired in them to do so.

The hospital was named after St. Ultan of Ardbraccan, County Meath, patron saint of paediatricians. Many of the founding members associated with St. Ultan's, such as Dr. Ella Webb, Dr. Alice Barry, and Dr. Lynn, were innovators in children's health. Dr. Webb was a pioneering Irish paediatrician and one of the founders of the Children's Sunshine Home for Convalescents (now LauraLynn Ireland Children's Hospice) a convalescence home for children with life-limiting diseases. Dr. Barry was an active and founding member of the Women's National Health Association (WNHA) which began in 1908. The WNHA became an integral organisation in Ireland's contribution to the war effort on the homefront and at the battlefront through its fundraising and organising of care packages for soldiers. Through the Health Association, Barry became the medical officer for nine Babies' Clubs in Dublin from 1912-1929. The Babies' Clubs aimed to educate mothers in the overall care of their infants by holding classes and lectures. There were over 170 Babies' Clubs set up across Ireland.

Many political figures were also present at the first committee meetings of St. Ultan's, such as Kathleen Clarke and Jennie Wyse-Power. Wyse-Power was a prominent member in the Ladies' Land League and Cumann na mBan and would become a Free State senator in the 1920s.

St. Monica's Babies' Club Dublin, opened in St. Augustine Street by the Dublin branch of the Women's National Health Association, 1909
(courtesy of Dublin City Library and Archives)

**Portrait of Dr. Kathleen
Lynn** (courtesy of the Royal
College of Physicians
Ireland Archives and
Heritage Centre)

Clarke, who was the widow of 1916 Rising leader Tom Clarke, was active in local
government and became the first woman elected Lord Mayor of Dublin in 1939.

The first meeting of the committee, which established the hospital, was primarily
concerned with providing much needed healthcare for infants and their mothers as
well as healthcare education for the public. The interweaving of public education
alongside healthcare provision was to be a core tenet of St. Ultan's ethos.

Under the leadership of Lynn, St. Ultan's soon developed into an important and
innovative paediatric hospital in Ireland and Britain. Lynn was born in 1874 in County
Mayo. Her father was a clergyman and her family moved around many parishes in
Mayo and Galway before settling in Cong, County Mayo in 1886. Growing up in the
west of Ireland in the aftermath of the Famine had a huge impact on Lynn who as a
child was impacted by the diseases and poverty suffered by the people in her local
area. This was a crucial influence on her desire to become a doctor after leaving
school. Lynn attended the Catholic University of Ireland's school of medicine in
Cecilia Street, Dublin, and the Royal College of Surgeons.

She graduated from Cecilia Street in 1899 and completed internships across the city including at Holles Street Hospital, the Rotunda Hospital, and the Royal Victoria Eye and Ear Hospital. She completed postgraduate work in the USA in the early 1900s before returning to Dublin to work as a duty doctor at hospitals in the city. She also established a general practice based in her home at 9 Belgrave Road, Rathmines, Dublin, where she lived from 1903 to 1955.

Photograph of the Royal College of Surgeons, overlooking St. Stephen's Green Park, 1916 (courtesy of Dublin City Library and Archives)

An active suffragist and an enthusiastic nationalist, Lynn was greatly influenced by labour activists like Helena Molony, Countess Markievicz and James Connolly. She worked in the soup kitchens during the Dublin Lockout of 1913, which brought her into close contact with impoverished families in Dublin. She joined the Irish Citizen Army (ICA) and taught first-aid to members of Cumann na mBan and the ICA. As chief medical officer of the ICA during the 1916 Rising, she tended to the wounded from her post at City Hall. She was one of many women detained in Richmond Barracks and then imprisoned in Kilmainham Gaol after the Rising. A committed socialist, she was an honorary vice-president of the Irish Women Workers' Union in 1917 and denounced the poor working conditions of many women workers. She became vice-president of the Sinn Féin executive in 1917, and her home was a meeting point for fellow Sinn Féin women, notably for meetings of Cumann na dTeachtaire (the League of Women Delegates).

Cumann na dTeachtaire became an important network for St. Ultan's in its early days. On the run between May and October 1918, she was arrested and sent to Arbour Hill detention barracks. The authorities agreed to release her, on the intervention of the Lord Mayor of Dublin, Laurence O'Neill, as her professional services were essential during the 1918–19 influenza epidemic.

Photograph taken in Liberty Hall the night Countess Markievicz was released from prison, Dr. Lynn is to the left of Markievicz, Ffrench-Mullen is beside Lynn, 15 March 1919 (courtesy of the National Library of Ireland)

St. Ultan's philosophy was to provide much-needed facilities, both medical and educational, for impoverished infants and their mothers. Under the leadership of Dr. Lynn the ethos of the hospital was patient-orientated. Lynn's holistic approach encompassed not only treating the cause of the illness with appropriate medicine, but also caring for and comforting the children by holding and soothing them. Lynn's interest in child-centred education was furthered in 1934 when Dr. Maria Montessori visited St. Ultan's. Throughout her life, Lynn preached the virtues of cleanliness and fresh air which she applied as much to her own life as to her medical practice. Her friend, the architect Michael Scott, designed a balcony outside her bedroom on Belgrave Road, where she slept for most of the year.

Despite the necessity for a dedicated children's hospital in Dublin, St. Ultan's struggled for funds. It started off with just two cots and its opening week was supported by a programme of theatrical events and lectures. 'St. Ultan's Week' ran from Saturday 24 to Saturday 31 May 1919 at the Abbey Theatre. The beautifully designed programme cover (opposite) includes an illustration of St. Ultan and the Irish name of St. Ultan's 'Teach Naoimh Ultuin', is prominently displayed underneath.

The front page reads: 'In aid of the new infant hospital, Charlemont Street, first and only infant hospital in Ireland.' Some of the key events for the week include a performance of *The Singer*, by P. H. Pearse (importantly, with the permission of his mother, Mrs. Margaret Pearse), and *An enemy of the people* by Henrik Ibsen. Fundraising continued throughout the life of the hospital with Ffrench-Mullen and Lynn sometimes visiting the USA to raise funds for St. Ultan's while incorporating visits to paediatric institutions as well.

Members of the National BCG Committee taken in St. Ultan's (Dr. Lynn second from left) visiting patients in the BCG unit, November 1951 (courtesy of the National Library of Ireland)

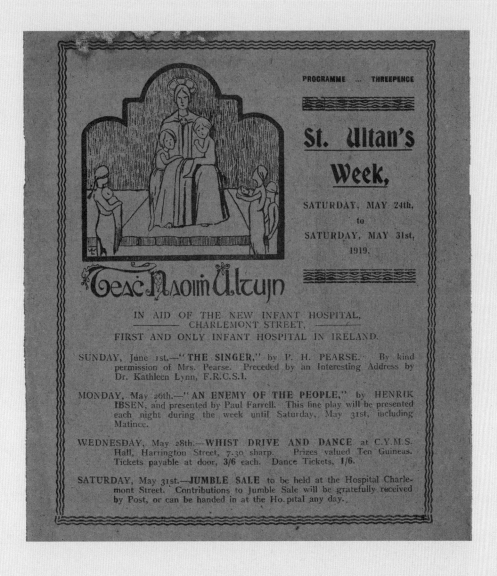

St. Ultan's Week: a fundraiser for the hospital in 1919
(courtesy of the National Library of Ireland)

'The "Civic" Searchlight, The Blight Being Nailed - Bad Housing Conditions
-Tuberculosis and Ignorance', *The Lepracaun Collection*, 1914
(courtesy of Dublin City Library and Archives)

THE "CIVIC" SEARCHLIGHT, THE BLIGHT BEING NAILED.

TUBERCULOSIS (to Ignorance): " Lord Glenconnor said last week that you were my greatest friend.   Sure every-
body knows that but yourself."
THE SEARCHLIGHT PARTY: " Ah! We've tracked them. Now to clear out the visitor and educate the entertainer."

During the early years of St. Ultan's, and well into the 1930s, the slums of Dublin were notoriously disease-ridden, where a high percentage of the population lived in one-roomed accommodation. The infant mortality rate and the rate of tuberculosis (TB) infection was much higher in these slums than many other cities in Western Europe at the time. St. Ultan's was at the forefront of new international research which sought to combat the disease with one doctor in particular proving crucial in helping to fight TB, Dr. Dorothy Stopford-Price.

Dorothy Stopford was born in 1890 into a well-connected Anglo-Irish family. Her aunt, Alice Stopford-Green, was an important historian of Irish history and a nationalist whose home at 90 St. Stephen's Green became an intellectual centre for the cultural revolutionary movement. In her early twenties, Stopford-Price developed an ardent republican outlook. Upon graduating with a medical degree from Trinity College, she was appointed medical officer in Kilbrittain in County Cork during the War of Independence. Coincidentally, Dr. Alice Barry, a founder of St. Ultan's, worked in Kilbrittain as the dispensary district medical officer until she was succeeded by Stopford-Price. In addition to her work in the medical dispensary, Stopford-Price trained members of the Irish Republican Army and Cumann na mBan in first-aid, and administered medicine to revolutionaries. The local battalion were very fond of her as she records in many of her letters home to her mother Constance during this period. Years after she had moved back to Dublin, they sent her a note congratulating her on her wedding to Liam Price in 1925.

As early as 1921, Stopford-Price began to channel her energies towards eradicating TB in Ireland. At a time when the Irish medical profession looked to the United Kingdom for leadership, she taught herself German to access scientific literature at the forefront of medical developments on the continent. Stopford-Price became acquainted with Kathleen Lynn during her time as a medical student in Dublin and worked as a house surgeon at St. Ultan's in 1923. Stopford-Price's specific interest in a TB vaccination grew out of her work in St. Ultan's, where she came into contact with poor families of the Dublin slums where the disease was rampant. Her work on TB tuberculin testing made it possible to establish whether a patient had TB or not and treat those who did. It turned out that a large proportion of the Irish population, particularly in rural areas, had never been exposed to TB, and therefore had no immunity to it. This made a vaccination programme all the more essential.

Stopford-Price established that in Ireland only 11 per cent of 14-year-olds had been exposed to TB whereas there was a high rate of tuberculin reaction among the same age group in Paris (75 per cent) and Denmark (56 per cent). Her work in tuberculin testing from the early 1930s, alongside Dr. Nora O'Leary, was important in that it disproved the belief among the medical profession that all young Irish adults had been exposed to tuberculosis. While she is especially associated with St. Ultan's, Stopford-Price also worked with the Royal City of Dublin Hospital, whose radiological facilities she used to research and diagnose children with TB.

Stopford-Price investigated international practices, and visited some of the pioneers of TB diagnosis and prevention, particularly in Scandinavia, where important advances had been made. Below is an image of the Municipal Bacteriological Lab in Gothenburg in Sweden run by the Swedish paediatrician Professor Avrid Wallgren. From the 1920s, Sweden introduced a universal vaccine of TB through the BCG vaccine (Bacillus Calmette-Guérin vaccine, named after two French scientists Albert Calmette and Camille Guérin who had developed it). The vaccine had been developed first in France as an oral vaccine, but it was the Gothenburg lab that introduced the method of injecting into the skin, which proved to be the most successful method. By the 1940s, the Gothenburg lab was providing the vaccine to hospitals in Germany, Britain and St. Ultan's in Ireland.

Municipal Bacteriological Lab in Gothenburg in Sweden, 1926
(courtesy of the National Library of Ireland)

Dr. Stopford-Price continued her study of international vaccine practices, and completed a postgraduate course in Bavaria in 1934. Stopford-Price began importing and testing the BCG vaccine in the 1930s, gathering support for a nationwide programme and publishing her findings in journals and textbooks. A major breakthrough for Stopford-Price came on 5 December 1936 when the Department of Health granted her a licence to import the BCG vaccine from Sweden. She could now introduce a pilot BCG programme to St. Ultan's. The two-year programme began with testing five infants with the vaccination in the Dublin area, with varying degrees of inoculation success. Plans for further testing were disrupted by the Second World War as it was difficult for Stopford-Price to import the vaccine from Sweden. Despite these difficulties, Stopford-Price continued to work and research, and her 1942 book *Tuberculosis in childhood* was widely and favourably reviewed both in the national and international medical community; a second edition was published in 1948. She was nominated for the World Health Organisation Leon Bernard prize for her contribution to social medicine.

Dr. Stopford-Price (left) with a nurse and a patient, May 1947 (courtesy of Trinity College Dublin Manuscripts Department)

By 1946 the TB unit at St. Ultan's had been extended and Stopford-Price noted that 'BCG is used exclusively at St. Ultan's, which is the first hospital in Great Britain and Ireland to use it.' Her work was recognised by Dr. Noel Browne, who had been appointed Minister for Health in February 1948, when the National BCG Centre was located at St. Ultan's in 1949 with Stopford-Price as its first chairperson.

The new purpose-built BCG unit in St. Ultan's, the first in the country, was opened on 20 June 1949. It consisted of offices and committee rooms on the ground floor, together with outpatients and tuberculosis clinics and a new radiological department. On the upper floor, there were twelve cots and an isolation cubicle.

The BCG Unit, St. Ultan's Hospital and Headquarters of the National BCG Committee (courtesy of the National Library of Ireland)

The unit was said to be 'the best designed clinic in these islands.' It was designed as a sun trap with balconies sheltered by an overhanging roof. An article in a nursing magazine enthused: 'The colour of the walls are all pastel and are very beautiful. One gets an extraordinary impression of light and space and complete transparency.' St. Ultan's had grown from a two-cot hospital in 1919 to a 90 bed hospital for children up to five years of age. In effect, the hospital dealt with as many TB cases as it did general cases. There were 47 cots for general medical cases up to two years; 30 cots for tubercular cases up to five years; and 13 cots for BCG vaccination up to five years.

Dr. Margaret, also known as 'Pearl', Dunlevy, collaborated with Dr. Stopford-Price during this period. Dr. Dunlevy spearheaded a childhood BCG vaccination scheme in Dublin run by the Dublin Corporation Primary Tuberculosis Clinic, established in 1945, in conjunction with the campaign run by St. Ultan's. The incidences of TB in the city, rising during the Second World War, peaked in 1947. Children under five years of age experienced the highest mortality; of the 138 childhood TB deaths in the city in 1947 (81 of which were due to tuberculosis meningitis), 101 were aged five years or under. Emanating from a Medical Research Council of Ireland committee (1946) tasked with assessing TB treatments and the utility of vaccination, the Dublin Corporation BCG vaccination scheme commenced in October 1948.

Initially focusing on newborn children of TB-infected parents, the scheme gradually expanded to include all newborn children, student nurses and medical students, and later the staff and students of residential schools. By 1949, with radiological screening rapidly identifying those in need of treatment at St. Ultan's, childhood TB deaths decreased to 46 (one-third of their 1947 total).

The first decade of the BCG campaigns coincided with the ending of the Irish tuberculosis epidemic. However, it also coincided with a number of other interventions, such as the development of effective antibiotic therapy, the provision of sufficient X-ray equipment in Ireland, and the increased availability of hospital and sanatoria beds and better housing and nutrition.

Despite all of its innovative and important work St. Ultan's was one of the many independent organisations that fell foul of the ongoing battle for control of health between Church and State. In 1943, the Catholic Archbishop of Dublin, John Charles McQuaid opposed Stopford-Price's attempt to set up an Anti-Tuberculosis League, something which existed in all other European countries. McQuaid did not like the fact that the proposed league had protestant members in controlling positions, and even a lone atheist, Owen Sheehy-Skeffington.

Family visit to St. Ultan's (courtesy of the National Library of Ireland)

21

Nonetheless, public campaigns continued and in 1949 Noel Browne appointed Dunlevy to the national BCG committee, with its headquarters in St. Ultan's. The committee worked to gradually expand BCG vaccinations nationwide at the same time as the Dublin scheme. Soon the implementation of the BCG vaccine was common practice for children across Ireland.

St. Ultan's closed in 1984 when it merged with the National Children's Hospital in Harcourt Street, later Tallaght Hospital. The site became part of the Charlemont Clinic, a private medical clinic which operated until 2014, when it was sold for redevelopment for a luxury hotel and apartment complex, retaining the protected structure at 37 Charlemont Street and those at 35 and 36 Charlemont Street.

St. Ultan's helped women doctors to make their mark in the medical world, whether this was in paediatric or other fields and part of its legacy for professional women was its use of innovation and the confidence it inspired in that early generation.

Staff of St. Ultan's Hospital Dr. Lynn is third from left, Dr. Stopford-Price is second from right in the back row, 1936 (courtesy of Trinity College Dublin Manuscripts Department)

Further Reading

- The diaries and papers of Dr. Kathleen Lynn, Royal College of Physician Archives.

- The Ffrench-Mullen papers, Allen Library.

- The Dr. Dorothy Stopford-Price papers, National Library of Ireland.

- BRYAN, DEIRDRE. *Madeleine Ffrench-Mullen*, Dictionary of Irish Biography.

- PRICE, LIAM (ED.). *Dr. Dorothy Price, An Account of Twenty Years Fight Against Tuberculosis in Ireland.* University Press, 1957.

- MAC LELLAN, ANNE. *Dorothy Stopford-Price, Rebel Doctor.* Irish Academic Press, 2014.

- Ó HÓGARTAIGH, MARGARET. 'St. Ultan's: A hospital for Women.' *History Ireland*, July/August 2005.

- Ó HÓGARTAIGH, MARGARET. *Kathleen Lynn*, Dictionary of Irish Biography.

- WHELAN, BERNADETTE, *Women and Paid Work in Ireland, 1500-1930*, Four Courts Press, 2000.

Séamus Ennis performing with young musicians on RTÉ's
Séamus Ennis sa Chathaoir, **1963** (courtesy of RTÉ Photographic Archive)

Séamus Ennis: An Fear Ceoil

James Curry, Historian in Residence, Dublin North West

2019 marks the centenary of the birth of Séamus Ennis, the renowned musician, singer, folklorist and broadcaster who left behind, to quote from one obituary notice, 'a priceless heritage of Irish tradition to the nation.' The centenary year saw a host of events take place across Dublin, including the unveiling of a Dublin City Council commemorative plaque at the site of his first home. To further mark the centenary, this chapter examines the life of a man regularly described as the ard-rí or high king of Irish pipers.

One of six children born to Dublin civil servant James Ennis and his wife Mary Josephine (née McCabe), who were married at the Pro-Cathedral two years earlier, James 'Séamus' Ennis was born at his two-storey home of Jamestown Lodge in Finglas on 5 May 1919. At the time Finglas was, 'a place of large farms and widely spaced houses,' to quote Ennis's mother (an accomplished fiddle player who hailed from County Monaghan), and he had a happy rural upbringing. Summer holidays were spent in the quiet village of Naul in north County Dublin, where his paternal ancestors had lived for several generations. Coming from a musical family, Ennis's father was a talented and versatile musician who would play the uilleann pipes to his son when he was an infant to help him drift off to sleep. He also played him tunes after he had been 'promoted upstairs to a bedroom from the cradle' and Ennis began to learn to play the pipes himself at the age of thirteen. Ennis was the only one of the family's children to take up music seriously.

After receiving his education at the Holy Faith Convent in Glasnevin, Belvedere College and Coláiste Mhuire, as a young man Ennis worked for family friend Colm O Lochlainn's 'The Sign of the Three Candles' printing house at Fleet Street in Dublin. It was here that he learned to write musical notation properly, a skill that proved extremely valuable in his subsequent career. Ennis was forced to move on from his printing house job due to paper shortages caused by the Second World War. But with O Lochlainn's assistance he was employed from 1942 to 1947 as a full-time collector for the Irish Folklore Commission, amassing the largest ever first-hand compilation of folk songs *as Gaeilge*.

His initial mode of transport as a collector was by bicycle. Ennis drew upon his stamina, patience, prodigious memory, charm and musical versatility to painstakingly collect an invaluable array of songs and lore which are now housed in University College Dublin's National Folklore Collection. The three bound volumes of his handwritten field diary, written mostly in Irish, have been translated into English and edited by Ríonach uí Ógáin in her book *Going to the Well for Water* (published in 2009). The following entries from June to August 1943, when Ennis was stationed in Connemara, demonstrate the type of work he did. They are a perfect example of how the Dubliner sometimes bonded with those he encountered on his travels:

SATURDAY 26.6.43

Went to Glinsce... and found Colm, who welcomed me heartily. Of all the people I have ever met, Colm Ó Caodháin is the person I most enjoy working with. He made me very welcome and was delighted to see me again. I spent a long time talking to him. I wrote material down from him while he was cutting turf. I left him at 9:30. He told me he would not be there tomorrow, as he was going to An Aird Mhóir visiting and 'maybe,' he said, 'to have a small round of drink.'

MONDAY 19.7.43

In Glinsce in the afternoon and at night. Colm [Ó Caodháin] still has plenty of material but the work is progressing slowly because he talks a great deal about any subject that arises. I like working with him, although he may be a slow speaker. I do not wish to hurry him, as he is very kind to me and I have decided that there is no solution other than to spend as much time as I can with him. He talks about every aspect of life and makes philosophical comments on them.

WEDNESDAY 4.8.43

Spent the day from eleven o'clock until eight o'clock with Colm [Ó Caodháin] again. I have not written his entire repertoire yet. He came to Carna with me on a personal matter. I bought him a few drinks, and while we were drinking, he thought of an old religious song – Focla Chríost ag an Suipéar Deireanach ['Christ's Words at the Last Supper']. I wrote it from him. He then gave me a list of some of his songs that I have not yet written down.

I said goodbye to him, because I have decided to set off and travel north to Donegal tomorrow. I was very lonely leaving Colm and he was lonely as well, because we are very friendly with each other. Colm is a man who is rough and hearty in his ways, but he could sit in company at a grand feast, say in the President's residence, without embarrassment or fear of embarrassing anyone with him, he is so courteous. I was sad leaving him and I look forward no end to seeing him again.

For the next decade of his life, Ennis worked as a broadcaster for Radió Éireann and the BBC. The Radió Éireann position as an outside broadcasting officer commenced in the autumn of 1947 and saw Ennis, along with colleague Seán Mac Réamoinn, travel around Ireland. They mainly went to Irish-speaking areas to 'give a sound picture of the district, the people, the way they lived, their homes.' Song texts and airs were collected, along with reels, jigs, slip jigs and dance tunes. Whenever called upon to present the music of others to the public, Ennis 'did so with an air of authority and with a voice which suited it down to the ground.' In November 1951 he left Ireland to take up employment with the BBC. This position, which lasted for seven years, came about after Donegal man Brian George, the Irish-speaking head of the BBC's Recorded Broadcasts Department, invited Ennis to London to collect folklore and music from across England, Wales and Scotland, as well as in Ireland and Brittany in France. During his time with the BBC, Ennis worked on the highly-rated radio programme *As I Roved Out* and occasionally socialised with the likes of Dublin author Brendan Behan and Belfast poet Louis MacNeice.

Séamus Ennis takes down notes from Colm Ó Caodháin at his farm in Glinsce, Co. Galway. Looking on is one of Ó Caodháin's children, 1945 (courtesy of the National Folklore Collection, University College Dublin)

Less than a year after moving to England, Ennis briefly returned to his native land to marry Margaret Glynn. Margaret was an air hostess from Liverpool who had Irish parents and was partly brought up in County Wexford. The wedding took place on 16 September 1952 at the tiny Dauros Church in Tuosist, County Kerry. Back in London, the couple had one son and one daughter. Christopher was born in 1953 and Catherine two years later, before the parents separated during the summer of 1959 when Ennis returned to Ireland.

Dublin City Council commemorative plaque, unveiled in Finglas on 3 May 2019

After a spell working for Comhaltas Ceoltóirí Éireann, Ennis embraced the nomadic life of a freelance musical artist. He regularly appeared on Telefís Éireann (including starring in the 1963-64 series *Séamus Ennis sa Chathaoir*, which saw him perform with aspiring young musicians), played at Rhode Island's Newport Folk Festival in 1964. He subsequently spent five months touring universities in the United States, and in 1968 named and became a joint patron of the newly founded society of Irish pipers Na Píobairí Uilleann. Three years later, Ennis moved into a flat on Pembroke Road in Ballsbridge with fellow piper Liam O'Flynn and his brother Michael. It was here that he recorded his *Pure Drop* and *Music at the Gate* (later reissued as *The Fox Chase*) albums on the same evening with only two retakes. The following year he relocated to a house in Terenure and went on to record the double album *Forty Years of Piping*. In 1983 O'Flynn, regularly referred to by Ennis as Ireland's greatest piper, recalled his mentor's musical style as follows:

Séamus was meticulous, as is evidenced in the precision and accuracy of his playing. His extraordinary ability to reform and reshape a tune so that it fitted the chanter perfectly sprang from a complete mastery and understanding of his instrument. He possessed great technical skill and brilliance, allied with a great depth of feeling. His taste was impeccable. He never aimed to impress by showing off; restraint and elegance were the hallmark of his piping.

The same year Irish music collector and uilleann piper Brendán Breathnach summed up Ennis's playing style and musical legacy in the following terms:

His style is best described as non-legato. It was never wholly open but the force and the thrust of the music was never interrupted or impeded by stuttering staccato movements... Séamus Ennis conducted no school or college of piping and yet he has influenced a multitude of pipers. He was prodigal in performance and has left behind a rich heritage of piping which will ever be a pleasure and an inspiration. As a piper he enriched and enlarged the living tradition and therein lay his most valued contribution to the cultural life of his country.

Liam O'Flynn, Seán Keane and Séamus Ennis performing on RTÉ's *The Humours of Donnybrook*, 1978 (courtesy of RTÉ Photographic Archive)

In 1975, Ennis settled in Naul to live out his remaining years on land which had once belonged to his grandparents. A countryman at heart who didn't suffer fools gladly, Ennis felt a strong attachment for the 'sleepy' village. He christened the plot of land where he lived in a caravan 'Easter Snow' after the slow air of that name which he was fond of playing on the uilleann pipes. Ennis continued to perform across Ireland and sometimes further afield, including a memorable appearance at the Royal Albert Hall in London in 1980. He regularly adjudicated at school 'Slógadh Gael-Linn' competitions, and enjoyed hosting his visiting children and close friends for sessions spent playing cards, exchanging stories and limericks, and performing songs and tunes.

Séamus Ennis, *Evening Press*, 6 October 1982 (courtesy of Dublin City Library and Archives)

After years of deteriorating health, Séamus Ennis passed away at home in his sleep on 5 October 1982. He was 63-years-old, with his last public appearance taking place at the Lisdoonvarna Folk Festival a few months earlier on 11 July. Ennis's funeral service took place at the Church of the Nativity in Naul, as friends and neighbours stood in the rain for almost an hour to greet the cortege which had been delayed in heavy traffic. Many well-known musicians and performers attended the funeral, and the broadcaster Séan Mac Réamoinn delivered a bilingual oration in which he spoke of his late friend's sincerity, prowess as a piper, and fidelity to north County Dublin and Ireland. He remarked that Ennis 'was always true to himself and his music and when he took a piece of music from Ulster or any part of the country, he ensured it lost none of its local qualities in his playing.' Mac Réamoinn was also quoted in one newspaper as saying 'Thank you James for what you brought to us, the sense of joy, of beauty, and of belonging.' To conclude the service Liam O'Flynn played a lament on the set of Coyne pipes given to him by his deceased friend and mentor, which had originally belonged to Ennis's father.

Shortly after the funeral a *Sunday Independent* journalist reacted indignantly, writing that:

> *Wasn't it the typical Irish gesture – a grand funeral for a man who for the last years of his life was almost totally neglected by those who should have known better?*

> *Seamus Ennis, folk music man supreme, was buried last week. He, more than any other, raised Irish folk music to international status.*

> *Since we pay such incredible lip service to Irish culture, Seamus Ennis should have been heaped with honours.*

> *He wasn't, in fact, in the last few years he was scarcely heard of. People would ask "Whatever happened to Seamus Ennis?"*

> *The sad fact is that he lived out his last years in a caravan in a field north of Dublin. I wonder how many of the hundreds who trooped to his funeral tried to help him during those years?*

Christopher and Catherine Ennis at their father's funeral, *Irish Independent*, 9 October 1982 (courtesy of Dublin City Library and Archives)

Liam O'Flynn playing a lament at the funeral of Séamus Ennis, *Evening Press*, 9 October 1982 (courtesy of Dublin City Library and Archives)

Yet, aside from this outburst, the press in Ireland paid warm tributes, with one *Irish Independent* journalist recalling a treasured personal memory:

> *My own favourite recollection [of Séamus Ennis] is of a warm summer day, back in the sixties, the sun glistening on the waters of the Shannon which flowed past the bottom of the back lawn of the Bush Hotel in Carrick-on-Shannon.*
>
> *There was a Fleadh Cheoil being held in nearby Boyle and a few of us had retired to the peaceful coolness of the river-side lawn. Among the small group sprawled on the grass were Seamus Ennis and Liam Clancy, who began to swop airs and songs. Seamus began to play "Donall Óg" on the pipes, then started to sing the words in Irish. At the end of the first verse Liam broke in, with a spontaneous English translation of the verse which Seamus had just sung.*

They both went through that long song, verse for verse, in Irish and English and with uilleann-pipe accompaniment. We were held spellbound by that display of musicianship and talent, which came so easily and modestly from both Ennis and Clancy. Even the birds were stilled that day in Carrick-on-Shannon.

Uilleann piper playing at the Dublin Street Carnival,
College Green, 1984 (courtesy of Dublin City Library and Archives)

Since his death, various efforts have been made to help keep Ennis's memory alive. Feeling that his friend had not received 'the recognition that he deserved for all the work he did down through the years for Irish culture,' Christy Moore composed a musical tribute entitled *Easter Snow*. The lyrics to this song featured in the official programme for the inaugural Séamus Ennis Festival which took place in Finglas in 1994, a week-long event organised with the approval of Ennis's family and relatives. The festivities also included the re-naming of a local road in Ennis's honour. On the same morning the Lord Mayor of Dublin, John Gormley, also unveiled a commemorative plaque – designed by Finglas sculptor Leo Higgins and stonemason Bobby Blount – nearby on Jamestown Road. This was the site of the house where Ennis was born and raised but, to use his own words, had been 'bulldozed out of existence' to make way for a factory during the 1960s. Traditional pipers played at both ceremonies and the annual 'Féile Shéamuis Ennis' continued to operate in Finglas for another three years.

BÓTHAR SHÉAMAIS MHIC AONGHASA
SEAMUS ENNIS ROAD

11

Seamus Ennis Road in Finglas, officially named on 1 November 1994

Vincent Browne's life-size bronze statue of Séamus Ennis, unveiled in Naul in October 2001 (courtesy of Séamus Ennis Arts Centre)

Thanks in large part to the efforts of Seán Mac Philibín, on 23 October 2001, the Séamus Ennis Cultural Centre (now the Séamus Ennis Arts Centre) was officially opened by Fingal county councillor Cathal Boland. The occasion witnessed the unveiling of a life-sized bronze statue of a smiling Ennis sitting with uilleann pipes in hand outside the Naul venue that is situated adjacent to the plot of land where he spent his final days. A visible reminder of the truth concerning an *Irish Press* journalist's observation in 1982 that while his death marked 'the end of an era', Ennis's memory would undoubtedly live on.

Séamus Ennis commemorative plaque, unveiled in Finglas on 1 November 1994
(courtesy of James Curry)

Séamus Ennis exhibition at Finglas Library, 2019
(courtesy of James Curry)

Further Reading

- Breathnach, Brendan. *Séamus Ennis. A tribute to the man and his music* in *Musical Traditions*, No. 1, Mid 1983.

- Cronin, Maurice. *Séamus Ennis.* Dictionary of Irish Biography, 2009.

- Gorham, Maurice. *Forty years of Irish broadcasting.* Talbot Press for RTÉ, 1967.

- Mitchell, Pat. *The dance music of Séamus Ennis.* Na Píobairí Uilleann, 2007.

- Sayers, Peig. *An old woman's reflections.* Oxford University Press, 1962 [Translated from Irish by Séamus Ennis, and introduced by W. R. Rodgers].

- Uí Ógáin, Ríonach (ed.). *'Mise an fear ceoil': Séamus Ennis – Dialann Taistil 1942–1946.* Cló Iar-Chonnachta, 2007.

- Uí Ógáin, Ríonach (ed.). *Going to the well for water: the Séamus Ennis field diary 1942–46.* Cork University Press, 2009.

Local revolution: Dublin Corporation and the War of Independence, 1919 to 1921

Bernard Kelly, Historian in Residence, Dublin City Library and Archives

Public memory of the War of Independence is often dominated by many well-known events in Munster such as the ambushes at Kilmichael and Crossbarry in County Cork, but Dublin too played a central role in the conflict. As seat of the British administration in Ireland, with a heavy police and military presence, it was vital that the Irish Volunteers – in this period becoming more popularly known as the Irish Republican Army (IRA) – contested control of the city and demonstrated that British control over Ireland was loosening. As Richard Mulcahy, IRA chief of staff, said, 'the grip of our forces in Dublin must be maintained and strengthened at all costs.' While the IRA was the driving force of the military struggle against British rule, a parallel political conflict was waged by republicans against the established order. This was fought on a national level, most spectacularly in the UK general election in December 1918 when Sinn Féin almost swept the moderate Irish Parliamentary Party (IPP) into extinction. But it was also fought on the local stage, and at the centre of local politics in the capital was the Corporation. Dublin Corporation was established by the Municipal Corporations Act of 1840, which reformed the system of local government in Ireland. The Act abolished all but ten of the municipal boroughs on the island to more accurately reflect the shifting demographic and economic trends on the island.

In the years before the outbreak of the War of Independence in 1919, Dublin Corporation leaned towards moderate nationalism and contained many prominent nationalist (IPP) figures. The noted artist Sarah Cecilia Harrison was the first woman to sit on the Corporation and was elected in 1912. Although an independent member, she usually followed the policy laid down by the IPP. Future 1916 insurgent, member of the first Dáil, and eventual leader of the Irish Free State, W.T. Cosgrave was elected in 1909 to the Corporation.

Éamonn Ceannt, the leader of the rebel garrison at the South Dublin Union during the 1916 Rising, was employed by the City Treasury as a clerk. He was one of those executed by firing squad in Kilmainham Gaol in the aftermath of the rebellion. The Rising itself eroded some of the moderate tendencies of the Corporation. Lord Mayor Laurence O'Neill spoke out against the destruction of the city centre and the consequent reduction in Corporation income. Other more radical members called for public votes of sympathy for those who had been killed while participating in the rebellion. Alderman Thomas Kelly, chairman of the Housing Committee, was arrested in the wake of the Rising, as was W.T. Cosgrave who had served under Ceannt in the Rising. At a council meeting in June 1916, members called for Kelly's release, but did not mention Cosgrave. This was probably due to the fact that, as historian Pádraig Yeates has pointed out, Kelly did not engage in armed rebellion against the state.

The First World War also undoubtedly radicalised Irish politics. It set the stage for the decline of the Irish Parliamentary Party, and the Corporation was not exempt from the disruptive effects of this global conflict. When the German spring offensive of March-April 1918 threatened to break through the Allied front line in France, the London government reacted to the resulting manpower crisis by extending military conscription to Ireland. This shifted public opinion away from the moderate nationalism represented by the IPP. At the height of the crisis, it was Corporation Alderman Lorcan Sherlock, himself a notable United Irish League (UIL) figure and former Lord Mayor, who called for an all-party conference opposing conscription to be held at the Mansion House in Dublin. This historic conference was held on 18 April and attended by members of the IPP, the Labour Party, and Sinn Féin. The subsequent general strike on 23 April 1918 was supported by Dublin Corporation employees.

Conscription provided a common cause which united all shades of nationalist and republican opinion in Ireland, albeit uneasily, and in this they were supported by the Catholic Church. Sharing a platform with the moderate faces of Irish nationalism gave Sinn Féin an invaluable opportunity to push itself into the public eye, but also lent it an air of credibility and respectability. But this co-operation between the various shades of Irish nationalism was only skin-deep. The IPP's ill-fated decision to support the British war effort meant that Irish voters turned away from it in droves. In the December 1918 general election, Sinn Féin won 73 out of 105 seats and dominated all constituencies except in the north-eastern corner of Ulster, predicting the eventual partition of the island. In Dublin, the Sinn Féin victory was almost total. Out of seven seats in the city, six were won by Sinn Féin candidates. These were republican heavyweights: Richard Mulcahy in Clontarf, Sean T. O'Kelly in College Green, Philip Shanahan in Dublin

Harbour, Joseph McGrath in St. James', Michael Staines in St. Michan's, Thomas Kelly in St. Stephen's Green and Countess Markievicz in St. Patrick's. Sir Maurice Dockrell was the exception, taking a seat in Rathmines for the unionists. Between 1919 and 1920, the same pattern repeated itself on a local level and Dublin Corporation, which had traditionally been dominated by the IPP, was gradually taken over by republicans.

The first shots of the War of Independence were fired in Soloheadbeg in County Tipperary in January 1919 when a party of Irish Volunteers ambushed and killed two Royal Irish Constabulary (RIC) constables. On the same day, Sinn Féin's 69 (of the 73 seats won, 4 people won 2 seats each) successful candidates who had been elected in the December general election but refused to take their seats in Westminster, formed the breakaway Dáil Éireann in the Mansion House.

While the country was rapidly changing around them, council meetings in 1919 were dominated, not by the national question, but instead by an old and seemingly insoluble Dublin problem: that of housing. The 1913 Housing enquiry found that 22,000 people in the city were living in dwellings unfit for habitation. It was estimated that 14,000 new homes were needed, at a cost of £3.5 million. In 1915, Alderman Thomas Kelly suggested that the government should remove wives and children of Irish soldiers 'from the horrors of life in dilapidated tenement houses.' During the First World War almost 1,000 tenement dwellings were closed down, but the lack of materials and labour meant that just over 300 houses were built in the city, putting severe pressure on the rental market and making many families homeless. In the wake of the conscription crisis in 1918, the new Lord-Lieutenant Lord French called for 3,000 soldiers a month, promising, 'as far as possible, that land shall be available for men who have fought for their country.'

By 1919 it was becoming clear to Dublin Corporation that the British government was not going to take action to alleviate the housing problem, but it was still an issue that was far beyond the resources of the Corporation. Plans for new housing schemes at Crabbe Lane, Spitalfields, Mary's Lane, Boyne Street, North Lotts, Newfoundland Street, Friends Fields and Millbourne were suggested, but these would incur costs of £10,000 in architect fees alone. On top of this, as the Corporation slowly but surely moved towards supporting those calling for a complete separation from Britain, the issue of accepting funds from the British exchequer became a problem.

While hostilities had broken out between the Irish Volunteers and the British forces in 1919, the violence reached a new level in 1920. Again Dublin Corporation was not immune from these developments.

This was reflected in the makeup of the council; in 1919, it had largely been dominated by nationalists who adhered to the UIL and IPP line, but by 1920 this had altered. Michael Staines, Sinn Féin TD and later first Garda Síochána Commissioner, was elected to the council in the Arran Quay Ward. In the Mansion House Ward, Hannah Sheehy-Skeffington was elected, while Jennie Wyse Power was successful in the Inns Quay and Rotunda Wards. Kathleen Clarke, widow of Tom Clarke, was elected from the Mountjoy Ward. W.T. Cosgrave was returned along with Alfie Byrne and J.V. Lawless in the North City and North Dock areas.

The new members of the council saw themselves as representing a new way forward; as Sean T. O'Kelly put it in his Bureau of Military History witness statement, 'Inside the Municipal council the Sinn Féin Party acted as a reform party. Up to the time of the formation of the Sinn Féin party, nepotism was rife everywhere in the Municipal services.' This mixture of long-standing rebels and new republican blood pushed the council away from moderate nationalism towards opposing British rule in Ireland. From February 1920, the tricolour was flown from the flagpole outside City Hall; given its proximity to Dublin Castle, this was interpreted as a gesture of defiance. Not long afterwards, the municipal council passed a motion calling the attention of:

> the peoples of other countries to the intolerable conditions under which the people of this country labour, as instanced by the arrest and deportation without charge or trial, of three Members of this Council, and other Irishmen, under Acts passed in wartime, and the continuance of which cannot be justified unless on the assumption that a state of war exists between the country and England.

1920 saw a sharp escalation in the war in Dublin, with the arrival of several companies of Black and Tans and Auxiliaries, and the subsequent formation of an IRA Active Service Unit (ASU) in the city. A wide-ranging curfew was imposed on Dublin, forbidding people to be on the streets between midnight and 5am. Most public buildings were fortified with barbed wire or sandbags, giving the impression of a city at war.

From the beginning of 1920 the Corporation itself and its members had come under increasing pressure from the police. By March 1920 council members such as Thomas Kelly, Joseph McDonagh, William O'Brien and John Forrestal had all been detained by the British forces. On 6 December 1920, a council meeting was raided by the Auxiliaries: the minutes of the meeting recorded that, 'the proceedings of the Council were interrupted by the entrance of armed forces of the Crown.'

They arrested Michael Staines, Thomas Lawlor, Kathleen Clarke, James Lawless, James Brennan and Michael Lynch. Lord Mayor Laurence O'Neill, no doubt worried by the Auxiliaries' reputation for brutality, immediately wrote to British Prime Minister Lloyd George, holding him responsible for the safety of the prisoners.

576

mentioned Minutes only were signed by the Right Hon. the Lord Mayor:

The Right Hon. the Lord Mayor stated that he would not sign the Council Minutes of the 4th. October, as they were not a full record of the whole meeting:

The Town Clerk (Mr. Campbell) stated that the Minutes of the 4th. October were correct:

It was moved by Councillor Captain McWalter, M.D.; and, seconded by Alderman James Hubbard Clark, J.P.:— "That the Minutes as circulated (4th. October) up to page 496, ending with the words 'Council Chamber,' be signed as correct:"

The motion was put; whereupon, the following amendment was moved by Councillor Forrestal; and, seconded by Councillor Loughlin:—"That the Minutes of the 4th. October be amended by the inclusion of everything which occurred at the meeting of the 4th. October:"

At this point the proceedings of the Council were interrupted by the entrance of armed forces of the Crown, who arrested Alderman Staines, Alderman Thomas Lawlor, and Councillors Clarke, Lawless, Brennan and Lynch.

It was then moved by Councillor P. T. Daly; and, seconded by Councillor Loughlin:—"That owing to what has happened, the Council adjourn to 14th. instant:" The motion was put and carried.

Correct:

MICHAEL J. WALSH,
Town Clerk pro tem.

Lord Mayor.

Dollard—O220 1. 1921 400.— Irish Paper.

Municipal council minutes, 6 December 1920 (courtesy of Dublin City Library and Archives)

The Corporation had become a target for the Crown forces because, in May 1920, the council transferred its adherence from the British Local Government Board to Dáil Éireann. Suggesting the change in allegiance, councillor Michael Dowling put forward a motion that the council:

> acknowledge the authority of Dáil Éireann as the duly elected Government of the Irish People and undertakes to give effect to all decrees duly promulgated by the said Dáil Éireann in so far as same affects this Council.

This was a crucial turning point in the political battle against British rule. Militarily, the IRA was contesting the Crown's control of the streets; in parallel, republicans were challenging the old order's hold on the political levers of power. Dublin Corporation's public support for Dáil Éireann was a major boost for the revolution. However, it did not pass without opposition: five councillors voted against it and the assistant to the town clerk stated his opinion that Dowling's motion was 'out of order' because it was illegal for the council to pass a resolution that contravened existing law. Eventually the town clerk Henry Campbell handed in his resignation in exasperation at the actions of Sinn Féin on the council. He complained about the, 'illegalities, irregularities and indecencies perpetrated or attempted to perpetrate by the councillors.' The council's decisive shift towards open defiance set the scene for several smaller battles between the Corporation and the British authorities, and the Local Government Board (LGB). In July 1920, the LGB wrote to the Corporation, pointing out that in order to qualify for funding, Irish local authorities had to, 'submit their accounts to audit and be prepared to conform to the rules and orders of the Local Government Board, as heretofore.' In particular, the letter warned that:

> many local authorities are engaged in the preparation of schemes for housing, road construction and public health improvements, all of which involve loans and large subsidies from the Imperial Exchequer. They, therefore, deem it right to give early intimation that unless the applications for the loans and grants from these Authorities are accompanied by an assurance, as aforesaid, it will not be within the discretion of the Local Government Board to entertain them.

This was followed by a letter in August 1920 from the Chief Secretary's Office in Dublin Castle, threatening to withhold tax revenue from any council that did not comply, and requesting that all local governing bodies open their books for official audit.

When it was suggested that the necessary assurances be supplied to the LGB, W.T. Cosgrave effectively sabotaged the motion by amending it to say that the letters had been read, but without the required pledges of loyalty to the LGB included. There then followed a game of cat and mouse between the LGB auditor and the republican members of the Corporation, who sought at every turn to block the accountants gaining access to the council financial records. In October 1920, the Dáil itself issued an instruction to the town clerk not to release any records to the LGB and that any audit would be carried out under the auspices of the Dáil's Department of Local Government. Eventually the British auditors successfully petitioned a judge to order the records to be released, with the penalty of contempt of court hanging over any member of the Corporation who refused to comply. Cosgrave got around this neatly by instructing:

> *Mr. Eyre, the City Treasurer and responsible officer, to collect all books and accounts necessary to the audit, and store them in the auditor's room ready for his use and inspection the following Monday. These instructions were carried out as directed. On the following day, Saturday, a raid was made on the auditor's office by Volunteer forces under the command of Joe McGrath and all books and accounts were removed. Counsel for the Corporation was now in a position to tell the Court that the Corporation had taken all necessary steps to facilitate the audit but that, owing to circumstances over which the Corporation had no control, the books and documents were no longer available.*

This convenient sleight of hand was assisted by the fact that Cosgrave was simultaneously a Sinn Féin TD, the Minister for Local Government in the first Dáil, and chairman of the Finance Committee of the Corporation. This running battle with the LGB auditors was therefore important to Cosgrave at both the local and national level. Locally it was vital to keep the Corporation outside the remit of the LGB, while nationally other county and city councils who had repudiated British authority looked to Cosgrave for leadership. However, this last confrontation provoked the British authorities into action. On 22 December 1920 City Hall was occupied by British troops, the tricolor pulled down from the flagpole and barbed wire placed across all entrances. Lord Mayor Laurence O'Neill made the Mansion House available to the council to hold its meetings; this was raided by the police on 17 May 1921.

City Hall being occupied, December 1920 (courtesy of Dublin City Library and Archives)

The war against the British ground slowly to a halt throughout the first half of 1921. On 14 March six IRA men were hanged in Mountjoy prison following courts-martial. On the same day Laurence O'Neill put a motion before the council expressing sympathy with the families of the deceased. He placed on record 'our admiration of the heroic fortitude with which they met their deaths for Ireland' and the council adjourned out of respect following this. Throughout 1921, unusual items became focal points of confrontation between the Corporation and the authorities. On 5 May 1921 Ernest Blythe, Dáil Minister of Trade, signed an order banning the importation or purchase of British margarine in Ireland, having previously prohibited the importation of British manufactured binders, mowing machines, rakes, ploughs, hay trollies, harrows, corn drills, root cutters, biscuits, boot polish and soap. Blythe's order was inserted into the minutes and referred to the Health Committee for action. While this was winding its way through the maze of local administration, on 25 May 1921 the IRA staged a disastrous assault on the Customs House, which saw five IRA members killed and almost 100 captured. The losses were so considerable that IRA activity dropped off significantly until the truce on 11 July.

As the war began to wind down following the Customs House attack, the Corporation became more involved in calling for a cessation of hostilities. Even this was hijacked by republicans on the council. Unionist councillor Michael J. Maxwell-Lemon moved a motion calling for a truce of one month, 'during which time all rioting and murder should cease, for the purpose of endeavoring to promote peace and goodwill amongst all Irishmen of every section.' This was amended by councillors Forrestal and Raul to Ireland's struggle, 'against an unscrupulous aggression on her National and cultural life' and suggested that, 'any peace to be permanent in Ireland must be based on the recognition of Ireland as an Independent State.' It concluded with the bold statement that, 'peace can be established immediately by the withdrawal of the British Armed Forces and that Dáil Éireann was the only national body that had the authority to negotiate with London.'

The truce that ended the War of Independence was signed at the Corporation's new home, the Mansion House, on 9 July 1921 and came into effect on 11 July. The Corporation, like Dublin itself and Ireland as a whole, underwent radical change between 1919 and 1921, slipping out of the control of the old political elite and into the hands of the separatists. Its offices were raided, its members arrested, interned and targeted for harassment by the British forces. It was eventually disbanded in 1924 by the Free State government but the republican tradition of representation continued: Constance Markievicz, Dr. Kathleen Lynn and Hanna Sheehy-Skeffington were all elected to the new Dublin County Council in 1925. Kathleen Clarke became the first female Lord Mayor of Dublin in 1939, just as another world war was breaking out.

Plaque at the Mansion House commemorating the truce, 11 July 1921 (courtesy of Dublin City Library and Archives)

45

Further Reading

* Dublin Corporation Minutes. Dublin City Library and Archive.

* GIBNEY, JOHN. *Dublin City Council and the 1916 Rising.* Dublin City Council, 2016.

* YEATES, PÁDRAIG. *A City in Turmoil: Dublin 1919–1921.* Gill & Macmillan, 2012.

A History of Lemon's Pure Sweets

Cormac Moore, Historian in Residence, Dublin North Central

An *Irish Times* article from 11 November 1955 referenced that in 1842, 'a young woman in a dark blue velvet cloak with open sleeve edges with grey fur to match her muff, and wearing a pale blue satin bonnet and dress pushed open the door of a little shop in Dublin's Capel Street. A young man in a clean white apron greeted her. Nobody knows the name of the young woman, but the man was Graham Lemon, steadily gaining a reputation throughout the city of his skill as a maker of bon-bons, barley sugar and such-like sweet meats.' Sweetmeats was a common name used for sweets in the 19th century. Years later, this story of Graham Lemon helping a young lady, was the inspiration for the design of the company's famous logo.

Family records state that Graham Lemon was born in Mountnorris in County Armagh in 1819. He grew up in Belfast before moving to Dublin to ply his trade as a confectioner. He married Mary Barkley sometime in the 1840s, with the first of their nine children, John, born in 1845. They lived above his shop at 102 Capel Street. What set Graham apart initially was that he made his sweets by hand with no assistance from anyone. He also began his business, 'with the policy that quality was of paramount importance; only the freshest, purest ingredients went into the making of his product.' Needing more space for the sweet-making operation, and pre-empting future demand, Graham Lemon moved his shop to 49 Lower Sackville Street (present day O'Connell Street) in 1847, a busy thoroughfare from which he would benefit from the 'carriage trade.' Sackville Street was called 'the finest thoroughfare in the world' where 'civil and uncivil servants' frequented.

Ireland at the time was experiencing its darkest period, in the grips of the Great Irish Famine. The famine had a devastating impact on Ireland, with over 1 million deaths as well as the mass emigration of about 1.5 million people. This mass emigration continued throughout the 19th and early 20th centuries, resulting in the halving of the Irish population from 8 million in 1840 to 4 million in 1900. Rural parts of Ireland were most affected, with many forced to move to cities like Dublin to seek aid.

"CIVIL AND UNCIVIL SERVANTS."
SACKVILLE STREET—The Finest Thoroughfare in the World—Every Sunday from 3 p.m. to 1 a.m.
We hear with pleasure that the British Army is to be reduced by 20,000 men ; it will be a serious loss to Dublin.

'Civil and Uncivil Servants' on Sackville Street – 'The Finest Thoroughfare in the World', 1906 (courtesy of Dublin City Library and Archives)

When he moved to Sackville Street, Graham Lemon put the name 'Lemon & Co.' on the fanlight over the door, and being a man proud of his craft, he named the premises 'The Confectioner's Hall.' At the new larger premises, Lemon installed machinery to make the sweets and hired staff to sell them in the shop. The machinery and processes were new to Ireland at the time. Lemon and Company is considered to be the first company in Ireland to manufacture confectionery on an extensive scale. The entire building on Sackville Street was used for the sweet-making operation; production, packaging and sales. The firm, proud of the purity of its product, used the slogan, 'You cannot eat a better sweet.' Passers-by stopped to look through diamond-paned windows at the little piles of sweetmeats he set out for exhibition, and Graham Lemon prospered.

In April 1850, a freak storm hit Dublin. A thunderstorm was followed by a shower of huge hailstones, some claiming they were, 'as big as hen's eggs.' They certainly were as large as the mint humbugs made by Lemon's. Within an hour, the storm had caused damage totalling £27,000 in the city. Lemon's shop did not escape – the charming diamond-paned windows were smashed into a heap of broken glass. But Graham Lemon turned his misfortune into an opportunity as the shop became the first shop in Dublin to have plate glass in the windows. It was considered remarkable then to see one whole sheet of glass in a shop window.

With a new enlarged display window on show, the business thrived. Customers sought Lemon's barley sugar and mint humbugs; others asked for the now-forgotten brown sticks called 'Bath pipe' for its health benefits, to remove 'coughs and colds.' People could also purchase 'Yellow Man' – one of the earliest kinds of rock, later to become the standard souvenir of many tourist resorts.

The largest boost to Lemon's came with the Great Industrial Exhibition of 1853. The Exhibition, so soon after the devastating famine, was an attempt to present a positive impression of Ireland. It was an opportunity to stimulate Irish industry and to show the country had a future, and a bright one at that. Modelled on the London Great Exhibition of 1851 in Crystal Palace, companies exhibited their offerings to large audiences from May to October 1853. The main venue for the Exhibition was Leinster House, current site of the Oireachtas. Queen Victoria and many of the British royal family attended the Exhibition and were particularly impressed with Graham Lemon's stand. Lemon surpassed himself at the Exhibition: as well as an entire separate stand demonstrating how sweets were made, his product-stand displayed samples of lozenges, sugar-covered comfits (dried fruit, nuts or spices coated with sugar candy), boiled and crystallized confections, and bon bons.

There was even a model of the Great Industrial Exhibition Building made out of comfits. Lemon showed the royal family the process of making sweets using steam, explaining that, 'the confectionery was coloured with cochineal and other substances... not injurious to health.' With the making of confectionery being such a new concept, some were made with, 'highly poisonous colouring matters.' Members of the public were warned, 'from using any articles of confectionery in which green or blue colours existed, as the great probability would be that such are coloured by highly poisonous agents.'

An advertisement for the Great Industrial Exhibition in Dublin in 1853 (courtesy of Dublin City Library and Archives)

While at the Exhibition in 1853, Queen Victoria bought many of Graham Lemon's products, especially made for her, which she gave to her children. Lemon kept, 'the banker's draft with which these sweets were paid for by the Queen, as a memento.' In her last visit to Ireland in 1900, the Queen, 'specially patronised Lemon and Co. for the Easter Novelties, and expressed her appreciation of their products.' With illustrious customers such as the British royal family, Graham Lemon's business grew from strength to strength throughout the British Empire and beyond. Pope Leo XIII was also believed to be an admirer of, 'the firm's best varieties of manufactured sugar.'

Christmas was a particularly busy time for the shop. Lemon's sold Christmas Trees and Christmas Boxes, 'filled with our Pure Confectionery.' They also supplied 'Crystallised Fruits, with Confectionery Suitable for Christmas Trees.' Even those who could not afford the products in Lemon's shop could enjoy the wonderful window displays from the street at Christmas time.

The shop also attracted the attention of thieves. In 1856, two 'juvenile delinquents' were arrested for stealing a glass case of sweetmeats from Graham Lemon's shop. The arresting police constable saw the boys, 'gazing wistfully at the confectionery displayed in the complainant's shop for a considerable time. At last, after a brief consultation, both of them went in, one seized the case, with which he was making off when he and his colleague were arrested by the constable.' One boy was sentenced to receive 24 lashes, and the other 12 lashes. In 1862, a man was sentenced to three month's imprisonment with hard labour for stealing a wooden packing case and two tin cases from Lemon's.

The success of the business made Graham Lemon a very wealthy man. He was able to buy new shops on Grafton Street and St. Stephen's Green. He started to buy property around the city of Dublin, including many buildings in Little Grafton Street, just off Grafton Street. In 1871, Little Grafton Street was renamed Lemon Street in his honour, the name it remains to this day. In 1865, Graham Lemon purchased a new residence for his family in Yew Park, Clontarf.

Lemon was an active citizen of Dublin. He was in favour of opening St. Stephen's Green to the public and attended meetings proposing the re-building of Carlisle Bridge (present day O'Connell Bridge). He became town commissioner of Clontarf. As town commissioner, he attended a meeting at the Bilton Hotel in May 1870 which had in attendance, 'a remarkable mix of Protestants and Catholics, Liberals, Conservatives, gentry and ex-Fenians.' Lemon was listed as a 'Protestant Conservative.' Isaac Butt was also in attendance. The Home Government Association, a precursor to the Home Rule movement, was initiated at this meeting. In 1882, Lemon was sworn in as a Justice of the Peace for County Dublin.

That same year, he suffered a personal tragedy with the death of his wife, Mary. He re-married two years later, to an American citizen, Isabelle Ross. He travelled to the USA on the ship the *Scythia*, and married Isabelle in New York in May 1884. He was 65 at the time whilst Isabelle was 23-years-of-age. The marriage lasted for just over two years as Graham Lemon died suddenly at his home in Clontarf in October 1886 at the age of 67. After his death, the estate in Yew Park was sold, as was much of his property in Grafton and Lemon Streets.

Lemon and Company remained under family ownership and management after the founder's death. His son, Thomas Owens Lemon succeeded him as managing director. Thomas Owens was a well-known athlete who became chairman of the Clontarf Baths. Like his father, he also became a town commissioner of Clontarf. He died at the age of 65 in 1917. By the time of Thomas Owens' death, Lemon and Company had retained its status as one of the largest firms of its kind in Ireland.

The O'Connell Monument on Sackville (O'Connell) Street, The Confectioner's Hall can be seen on the left (courtesy of Dublin City Library and Archives)

During the First World War, 'when sugar and other ingredients were scarce, the Confectioner's Hall kept the quality of their goods up to their usual high standard, and made their sweets as good and as pure as before, even though it meant limited supplies.'

The Confectioner's Hall found itself close to the epicentre of the 1916 Easter Rising, being just doors away from the General Post Office. Lemon's also had a shop at 67 Middle Abbey Street. Whilst fortunate not to suffer the same fate as those premises that were burned during the week-long rebellion, the shops with their tasty treats on display became a target of looters who took advantage of the situation created by the rebellion during its first three days. Lower Sackville Street became a focal point for looting, where people stole toys, tobacco, hats, boots and food. Sugar was a target too with Lemon's and Noblett's sweet shops among the first shops to be looted. 'High-class sweets, toffees, Turkish delights, marzipans, crystallised fruits, fruit pastes and unsold Easter chocolate eggs' were taken from Lemon's and Noblett's. In one of the earliest accounts written of the Rising, *The Insurrection in Dublin*, the author James Stephens described in some detail the lure of the sweetshops for poor children:

> *Very many sweet shops were raided, and until the end of the rising
> sweet shops were the favourite mark of the looters. There is something
> comical in this looting of sweet shops – something almost innocent and
> child-like. Possibly most of the looters are children who are having the
> sole gorge of their lives. They have tasted sweetstuffs they had never
> toothed before, and will never taste again in this life, and until they die
> the insurrection of 1916 will have a sweet savour for them.*

After the Rising, Lemon and Company made a compensation claim of £1,063, 3 shillings
and 8 pence for damage to buildings and contents. It was awarded £630. Once the
upheavals of the Easter Rising and the First World War were over, Lemon's retained
its stature as one of Dublin's leading businesses. It soon became immortalised by
James Joyce in his novel, *Ulysses*. To Leopold Bloom, Lemon's is a place of:

> *Pineapple rock, lemon platt, butter scotch. A sugarsticky girl shovelling
> scoopfuls of creams for a christian brother. Some school treat. Bad for
> their tummies. Lozenge and comfit manufacturer to His Majesty the
> King. God. Save. Our. Sitting on his throne, sucking red jujubes white.*
>
> *A sombre Y.M.C.A. young man, watchful among the warm sweet fumes
> of Graham Lemon's, placed a throwaway in a hand of Mr Bloom.*

**The corner of Sackville (O'Connell) Street and Eden Quay after the
1916 Easter Rising** (courtesy of Dublin City Library and Archives)

Lemon's also appeared in a less well-known novel, *The Wheel of God* by George Egerton, pseudonym of Mary Chavelita Dunne from Laois, written in 1898. The novel's heroine Mary Desmond sees Graham Lemon's shop as a 'fairyland of sugar plums' and a 'kingdom of lollypops.'

By the 1920s, the Confectioner's Hall became too small for the manufacturing of sweets, such was the demand. A new factory was built in 1926 along the river Tolka at Millmount Place in Drumcondra for the mass production of Lemon's sweets. Six years after the Drumcondra factory was opened, its production capacity was doubled. That same year, 1932, the factory was the scene of a fatal accident. Just weeks before Christmas, an employee, 30-year-old Denis Deegan was putting a fan belt on one of the machines. Until then, it was not a requirement that machinery be stopped for such routine maintenance work. His clothes got caught between the belt and a revolving wheel. His two arms and left leg were almost torn from his body. By the time he was taken to the Mater Hospital, he had died.

The first Irish Free State government of Cumann na nGaedheal introduced a tariff on confectionery products coming into Ireland from abroad in 1924. This provided a massive boost to the sector in Dublin which led to a number of new firms establishing operations in the city.

Lemon's Factory in Drumcondra (courtesy of RTÉ Photographic Archive)

Urney Chocolates moved its production from Tyrone to Tallaght in 1924, employing 200 people there by 1928. Liam Devlin, whose pub on Parnell Street had served as a meeting place and safe-house for Michael Collins's intelligence team during the War of Independence, set up a new sweet factory on Gloucester Street (now Sean McDermott Street) in 1924 called the Triumph Toffee Works. Another sweet factory was established in Drumcondra by Joseph Milroy. Milroy's produced the much-loved macaroon bar. From 1924, British firms started to open operations in Dublin too. In 1926, Rowntree took over Savoy Confectionery of Inchicore. Similarly Macintosh bought out the North Kerry Manufacturing Company and built a new factory in Rathmines. Both firms subsequently merged to form Rowntree Macintosh. The UK firm Crosse & Blackwell took over Williams & Woods on Parnell Street in 1928 and in 1933, Cadbury's opened its first Irish factory on Ossory Road, North Strand.

Speaking at a dinner to celebrate 100 years in existence in 1942, Thomas Tate, the managing director of Lemon's, admitted the company had a 'rough time' in trying to meet the 'competition from England.' The firm's centenary was celebrated quietly as the world was at war. Ireland experienced much rationing and shortages. Output was cut sharply and queues formed along O'Connell Street for sweets from Lemon's. Sometimes the people at the end of the queue were disappointed as supplies had run out. Once the Second World War was over, the windows of Lemon's began to take on a brighter tone – new wrappings were being used to enrobe the sweets, and at the Drumcondra factory, machines from Switzerland, Germany, France, Britain and America were introduced into the manufacturing process. Electricity had replaced the older methods but still the basic ingredients were the same – sugar, butter and full cream milk. The machines poured out sweets – wrapped and foiled for freshness – at the high rate of 600 a minute per machine. Lemon's looked to maintain its competitive advantage by still sticking rigidly to its mantra of insisting on the highest quality for its products. On the factory floor, there were notices in red letters reminding everyone, 'This is a Food Factory – Cleanliness is Essential.'

Lemon's was also a great innovator in advertising. In the 1920s it was one of three companies to produce film commercials, as well as using more traditional modes of advertising in newspapers and at theatres. In the 1940s through to the 1960s, Lemon's Pure Sweets advertisements were a regular feature in newspapers. The slogan, 'This is Saturday, this is Lemon's Day' was well-known in the Irish advertising industry. Displays in the flagship store on O'Connell Street remained an enduring feature of Lemon's. The shop operated there until it was sold in the 1960s.

O'Connell Street with The Confectioner's Hall to the left, 1963
(courtesy of the National Library of Ireland)

The factory in Drumcondra continued to manufacture Lemon's sweets and was a regular source of employment for people in the area. Many of the employees were women. People remember the women in their white coats throwing sweets to the children gathered at the gates at the end of working days. Former Taoiseach, Bertie Ahern who grew up close to Lemon's factory, recalls in his autobiography, standing, 'outside the window calling to the girls to throw out broken toffee. They would make the Easter eggs about a month early, so we would all be bundling after the chocolate and scoffing ourselves.'

Whilst most locals were happy with the employment and free sweets offered by Lemon's, some residents complained of the pollution emanating from the factory. One resident brought Lemon's to court in 1967 seeking, 'damages for nuisances caused by soot and smuts from a chimney stack in the sweet factory.' Residents complained of clothing on washing lines in gardens being soiled and soot lodging like 'black hailstones' on cars and timberwork. Some cars were, 'completely covered with an oily deposit of soot.' The problem was considered, 'a grave danger to health in the neighbourhood.'

The Confectioner's Hall, 1969 (courtesy of Dublin City Library and Archives)

The high tariff walls of the 1920s that allowed indigenous confectionery companies to survive in Ireland disappeared during this time. Producing a large variety of products for a small market with no economies of scale saw the closure of many Irish confectionery companies. Lemon's struggled too. It was bought by British firm Barker & Dobson but it was clear by the late 1970s that the company was in serious trouble. In 1979, an agreement was reached that the tea and snacks firm, Irish Tea Merchants (ITM) Ltd., would take over the marketing and distribution of Lemon's whilst Barker & Dobson continued to run the Drumcondra factory as a production unit, saving 130 jobs in the process. ITM, which also marketed KP snack foods and Robert Roberts catering brands, subsequently bought the Lemon's brand name in August 1982. A month later, Barker & Dobson sold Lemon's to a German group called SBG in an attempt to save the Drumcondra factory. Under the deal, 28 of the 103 workers were made redundant. The attempted rescue plan did not work and the factory finally closed its doors in 1983. The factory has since been demolished, making way for a housing development.

The brand name Lemon's has survived and is now owned by Valeo Foods. You can find it on sweets such as Iced Caramels, Orchard Jellies, Chocolate Macaroons and the favourite, Season's Greetings is still on sale each Christmas. At 49 Lower O'Connell Street, some letters of the Confectioner's Hall sign have gone, but it is still clearly visible. In the words of Graham Lemon's descendant, Mary E. Lemon, 'even though the company, the shop and the factory no longer exist, what has endured for 175 years, is the Lemon's brand; a testament to one man's dream, and his reputation for quality, which he achieved through hard work and a principled philosophy.'

Further Reading

* *History of Lemon's Sweets* by Mary E. Lemon

* AHERN, BERTIE. *Bertie Ahern: The Autobiography*. Arrow, 2010.

* BARRY, FRANK. *The Leading Manufacturing Firms in 1920s Dublin*. Presentation delivered to Old Dublin Society, Pearse Street Library, 13 September 2017.

* DELEUZE, MARJORIE. *1916: Dublin Youths' Sweet Revolution*. Dublin Gastronomy Symposium – Food and Revolution, 2016.

* DIXON, F.E. *Dublin Exhibitions: Part I*. Dublin Historical Record Vol. 26, No. 3 June 1973.

* GOLDEN, J.J. *The Protestant Influence on the Origins of Irish Home Rule, 1861–1871*. The English Historical Review Vol. 128, No. 535 December 2013.

* HART, ANTONIO. *Ghost Signs of Dublin*. The History Press of Ireland, 2014.

* MALONE, BRENDA. *Toffee Axe, Looting in Dublin, 1916 Rising*. The Cricket Bat That Died For Ireland Blog, available at *https://thecricketbatthatdiedforireland.com*.

* STANDLEE, WHITNEY. *George Egerton, James Joyce and the Irish Künstlerroman*. Irish Studies Review Vol. 18, No. 4 2010.

* STEPHENS, JAMES. *The Insurrection in Dublin*. Maunsel & Company, 1916.

Back view of the buildings on Bishop Street before demolition to make way for Jacob's Biscuit Factory, 1891 (courtesy of Dublin City Library and Archives)

Disappearing workplaces: the changing face of Dublin in the 20th century

Mary Muldowney, Historian in Residence, Dublin Central

Many Irish communities have grown up around workplaces, whether that is in the shape of housing built specifically for the employees of a particular enterprise or clusters of people coming together to get access to a necessary resource like water or a raw material. Work, and the availability of it, is one of the essential features of human society and it has a huge impact; on the individual, on the community and its identity, and on the shape of the physical environment in which communities are situated.

In Dublin, there were several cases of housing being provided in the 19th and early 20th centuries for the employees of large enterprises such as the docks or railways or private companies like the Guinness Brewery. The need to have workers close to the business dictated how the areas developed. The city has expanded enormously since the beginning of the 20th century and many of the industries that were providing employment at that time have changed; either disappearing altogether or adapting to technological and other developments in the intervening century.

According to the 1901 Census, the main sources of male employment in Dublin were building, brewing, distilling, dockside labour, printing, the clothing trades, and various occupations serving the railways. A significant number of male workers had jobs as casual labourers and messengers, employed or laid off at will. Female employment was primarily concentrated in domestic service, although Jacob's Biscuit Factory was the city's most important employer of women at that time, with over 2,000 workers, many of whom lived close to the Bishop Street premises. There was no equivalent employer for the northside of the city, although in 1915 the opening of the National Shell Factory at Parkgate Street provided temporary jobs for almost 1,000 women during the First World War. Arnott's Department Store was the employer of the largest number of women on the city's northside.

This chapter will focus on a few individual case histories that illustrate how some workplaces still exist, but the work that was done in them has changed beyond recognition, while others have been erased from the physical landscape.

Dublin Metropolitan Cattle Market, 1926
(courtesy of Dublin City Library and Archives)

The Dublin Metropolitan Cattle Market

The history of Dublin's cattle market is an illustration of this process. The cattle market in Smithfield, on the northside of the city, was set up in the late 17th century and the sight of cattle being moved through the local streets was a common one. A new cattle market, called the Dublin Metropolitan Cattle Market, was officially opened in the Aughrim Street/Prussia Street area (Stoneybatter) in 1863 and it became the major point of sale for cattle. According to the census records from both 1901 and 1911, most male employment in the Stoneybatter, Smithfield and Markets areas was tied into the cattle business, between the market and the associated businesses.

During the early years of the 20th century this market was the busiest of its kind in Europe; throughput in 1917 alone numbered nearly three-quarters of a million animals. The Thom's Directories from those years show that there was a cluster of dealers' and auctioneers' offices on Prussia Street and Manor Street. These were men such as cattle dealer Owen Kenny, who lived at 36 Prussia Street and also had his offices there. According to the 1901 census, he was 48 years old and his wife Ellen was 24. The couple had two female servants: Mary Smith and Mary Brennan, aged 13 and 20 respectively.

The house no longer stands on Prussia Street but in its day, it was quite substantial, as the Census House and Building Return shows there were eleven rooms occupied by the family, in addition to seven 'outoffices.'

Other businesses associated with the cattle trade were abattoirs and butcher shops. The workers in these businesses were eligible to occupy some of the many houses in the area that had been built by the Dublin Artisans' Dwelling Company because they had steady jobs and could supply references. The Dublin Artisans' Dwelling Company had been started in 1876 by some members of the Dublin Sanitary Association. Sites that were already cleared by Dublin Corporation under Public Health Acts and the Artisans' and Labourers' Act of 1875 were then leased to the company and red brick one-storey cottages and two-storey houses were built.

As stated in the *Memorandum and Articles of Association of the Dublin Artisans' Dwellings Company Limited*:

> *Two references were required before a tenant could occupy a building; the tenant also had to be in steady employment... The company's first report states that it was working on thoroughly sound commercial principles and not as a charitable undertaking. By 1907 there were 2,961 dwellings housing 2,884 families or 13,330 individuals. Each house had a water supply, a yard and water closet.*

Thom's Directory also shows a number of small hotels and guesthouses situated in the streets surrounding the cattle market. These provided accommodation for the cattle dealers and buyers, many of whom came from outside the city.

Cattle sales were the primary business of the area and the market in Prussia Street was the final sales point for close to 90 per cent of stock exported each year from Dublin. In the days preceding a sale, cattle, pigs and sheep were driven to the market, where they were assessed by the salesmen. From the cattle market, the livestock were shifted by local drovers or cattle drivers into yards around Prussia Street, before being finally moved back from the holding yards (lairages) into the market on the morning of the sale. Once they were sold, the livestock were driven along the streets to the nearby abattoirs or down the quays to the docks at North Wall to be exported live to England or the continent.

The Docks, North Wall, Dublin, 1945 (courtesy of Dublin City Library and Archives)

The prominence of the Dublin Cattle Market began to fade within the meat industry in Ireland and revenue steadily declined in the years after the Second World War. The situation was not helped by the impact of the bovine tuberculosis eradication campaign, which meant that only cattle attested as clear could be sold in the market. In the ten years from 1960, the throughput had declined by 80 per cent and by the 1970s the cattle market had closed down. The Drumalee housing estate was then built on the site and these days the thriving businesses in the area are shops, cafés and restaurants while the Grangegorman area houses the Technological University Dublin (formerly the DIT).

The Docklands

When the Custom House opened in 1791, Ringsend was the only built-up area near it. The remainder of the docklands area consisted of low-lying wastelands, which had been divided into lots – or lotts – by the Ballast Office. As Dublin port expanded downriver, this land became more valuable. People and businesses moved into the docklands, attracted by the prospect of jobs and the large tracts of underdeveloped land. The road from Ringsend to the city was regularly under water at high tide, but land was gradually drained or reclaimed.

To construct the North Wall and Alexandra Basin the port authority had to reclaim a large area of the foreshore, and this provided sites for factories and other businesses.

The population of the area increased steadily throughout the 19th century, and the vacant land was gradually covered with houses and commercial properties. Hotels, warehouses, coal yards and cattle yards moved near the port and railway lines ran through the area. Stables for the countless horses that transported goods from the port throughout the city were also located there.

Some of the larger employers, like the railway companies, built houses for their workers. Speculative builders erected small cottages in the lanes and back streets to cater for the rising population, but commercial and industrial development took precedence and the houses were occasionally demolished to provide sites for warehouses or other business premises and housing standards were poor.

From its origins until the late 20th century, the docklands area was always vulnerable to global economic changes. Thriving trade resulted in a bustling port and docklands, with workers, or dockers, required to unload ships' cargoes manually. But the reverse was also true as the prosperity of the area fluctuated in response to external economic conditions. The population also fluctuated in line with the rise and fall of trade as workers moved in or out as demand for their services waxed or waned.

Street facing onto South Docks, Dublin (courtesy of Dublin City Library and Archives)

In the second half of the 20th century, the nature of shipping changed dramatically and by the end of the 1970s containerisation had almost completely eradicated the need for dockers. Cargo can be transported in shipping containers that are interchangeable between ships, trains and trucks, using standardised handling equipment, reducing the need for dock workers to manually unload ships. This process is known as 'Ro-Ro', referring to the roll on, roll off nature of containerised shipping. What was a thriving industry with many employees has been replaced to some extent, as have many of the buildings in which those employees were housed. The docklands is now also a centre of digital technology, full of modern buildings that exemplify the altered purpose of the workplaces in the area.

Dublin docks, 1963 (courtesy of Dublin City Library and Archives)

**The Gasometer,
Dublin docks, 1960s**
(courtesy of Dublin City
Library and Archives)

Some of these modern buildings have been constructed on the sites of what was once another thriving industry in the docklands area, the city's gas industry. In 1866, the Dublin Gas-Light Company and four other private gas companies were amalgamated into the Alliance & Dublin Consumers' Gas Company. The company grew rapidly to be the dominant force in supplying Ireland's coal-gas market and continued to do so for the next 100 years. From 1889 onwards, they had a monopoly on public and private electric lighting throughout the southside of Dublin, replacing the oil lamps that had previously provided indoor and outdoor lighting. Gas quickly became the preferred fuel of Dublin's middle class, particularly for their cookers and stoves. The increased lighting also meant that the streets became safer, enabling people to feel more at ease, while the possibility of being able to read and write by gaslight at night provided a huge boost to education.

The Dublin Gas Company originally had its principal wharfage along the quaysides of the Grand Canal Docks. Colliers from Liverpool delivered increasingly large quantities of the coal that was required to make city gas. City or town gas was produced from the chemical reaction induced by heating large amounts of coal in airtight conditions, turning it into coke and capturing the gas that resulted from the process. The docklands also had an abundance of water, an important raw material in the coke-making process. When the company's coal requirements increased, it transferred wharfage operations to Sir John Rogerson's Quay on the southside of the Liffey, which was better placed to take larger coal ships.

The most visible thing about gasworks from early in the 20th century until the arrival of natural gas was the gas holders or 'gasometers', as they were known. For many years, the skyline of Dublin's southern docks was dominated by the 82.4m (252ft) high Gasometer, which was situated on the corner of Macken Street and Sir John Rogerson's Quay. Completed in 1934, the Dublin Gasometer had a capacity of 3 million cubic feet of gas (c. 85,000 m3). Office buildings occupy the site now.

An entire industry developed around the by-products of coal-gas production. They provided the raw materials for the chemical industry in the 19th century and the first half of the 20th century. Gas works were the first large-scale sources of ammonia, sulphur and sulphuric acid as well as providing tar for caulking roads and creosote for wood preservation. The latter was a liquidised by-product of the tarry substance created by burning coal. Its qualities made it effective for preserving timber but it is highly toxic and its production is now strictly controlled. Many early drugs and chemicals were also derived from by-products of gas.

Natural gas from Kinsale reached Dublin in 1982. After the district-by-district conversion of all gas appliances to enable them to use this new fuel directly, the Dublin Gasworks ceased production in 1986. Following extensive decontamination the gasometer was demolished in 1993. It would possibly have been demolished earlier but for the arrival of two peregrine falcons who decided to nest on its roof.

Jacob's Biscuit Factory

Two County Waterford brothers, W. and R. Jacob established a biscuit-making company in 1851 in Waterford. Some years later they took out a lease on premises at 5 & 6 Peter's Row, Dublin, later moving to Bishop Street, on the southside of the city where they created jobs for thousands of workers, many of whom were women.

The factory's operation in Bishop Street was distributed over eight floors. The staff facilities included a roof garden, separate male and female dining halls and medical care. The factory had its own packing and printing departments, which produced packaging for the biscuits and made crates for overseas shipment, among other activities, with packaging changing to keep up with changing styles. The ovens were on the ground floor and other elements of the biscuit baking processes were distributed throughout the building, including icing, chocolate-making and sugar-boiling. Jacob's regularly introduced new products. Some lines like cream crackers never lost their popularity but occasionally a brand of biscuit would cease production.

In 1911, Delia Larkin, sister of trade-unionist Jim Larkin, began a campaign to organise Dublin's women workers for better conditions, and Jacob's employees were included. She was the first public figure to draw attention to some of Jacob's undesirable employment practices, including low pay. She protested against the company's unfair punishments and exposed corruption in the management, concluding:

> Jacob's & Co. have no qualms of conscience whatever as far as the workers are concerned; they are out to make a profit, and make it they will, even though it be at the cost of ill-health and disablement to the girls, women, and men of Dublin.

During the Dublin Lockout in 1913, Jacob's summarily dismissed anyone who wore an Irish Transport & General Workers Union badge. The badges indicated the worker's determination to belong to the union of their choice, and many of those dismissed in Jacob's were women. Rosie Hackett, after whom the bridge between Marlborough Street and Hawkins Street is named, was one of the union organisers who was not reinstated in her job in Jacob's after the Lockout.

Jacobs had houses for their workers and employed a doctor and dentist in the factory. In the early 20th century, such welfare measures were significantly ahead of their time and were more typical of the Quaker ideals espoused by the Jacobs brothers than their refusal to pay decent wages or to deal with the union representatives elected by their employees.

Jacob's Biscuit Factory employees' staff photograph, 1890s (courtesy of Dublin City Library and Archives)

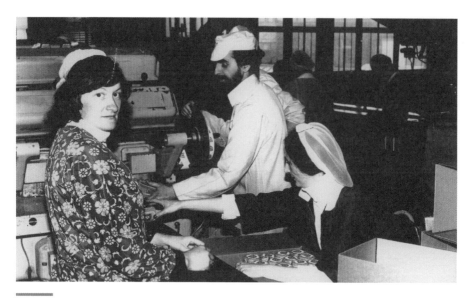

Last packing, Jacob's Biscuit Factory, Bishop Street, 1976
(courtesy of Dublin City Library and Archives)

The Bishop Street factory was vacated by Jacob's in 1976, when they moved to a new plant in Tallaght. In 2008, after 156 years of making biscuits in Ireland, Jacob's closed its Tallaght plant with the loss of 220 jobs and moved production to England. The empty building on Bishop Street was badly damaged by a fire in 1987 and was taken over by the Dublin Institute of Technology and is now home to the National Archives of Ireland.

D-Light Studios Building

An example of a workplace whose original purpose has long been overtaken but which continues to be a site of employment, albeit in a dissimilar manner, is D-Light Studios on the corner of Dunne Street and North Great Clarence Street on the city's northside. In 1900 John Wallis and Son, mail-cart contractors, general carriers, railway and steam packet agents occupied this building. The Wallis company had been involved in one of the most significant disputes in Irish industrial history, the 1913 Dublin Lockout. It was one of the main transport firms in the city, with two hundred horse-drawn vehicles lying idle once the strike began in August 1913. After a partial settlement of the strike had been reached in January 1914, Wallis and Son took back only a very small number of carters.

They carried on at this site until 1933, when the business went into liquidation. The building was then sold to the Great Southern Railway and by 1960 it was owned by a wool distribution company. That business continued until the 1970s, and for the next 30-odd years until 2017 when D-Light Studios took over, there was a series of auto factors and mechanic businesses in the premises. Today, the re-purposing of the building to house an arts studio and café keeps an old industrial building in use and is evidence of the movement from industrial to service employment in much of the city.

There is great value in everyday objects like machinery, photographs, tools and of course buildings to remind us of industrial processes and working methods that may no longer exist but which were of considerable importance in their day. The industrial change that transformed much of our city has made itself felt in even the small number of examples cited in this chapter. Humans adapt to changed circumstances but there are frequently casualties in the process. We can respect their memory by preserving our industrial heritage and stories.

Rear view of D-Light Studios on Dunne Street, looking towards the corner of North Great Clarence Street, 2018
(courtesy of Mary Muldowney)

Further Reading

- Brady, Joseph and Angret Simms (eds.). *Dublin Through Space & Time 900–1900*. Four Courts Press, 2001.

- Bunbury, Turtle. *Dublin Docklands: An Urban Voyage*. Montague Publications Group, 2009.

- Dickson, David. *Dublin. The Making of a Capital City*. Profile Books, 2014.

- Gilligan, Harry. *A History of the Port of Dublin*. Gill & Macmillan, 1989.

- Pearson, Peter. *The Heart of Dublin. Resurgence of an historic city*. O'Brien Press, 2000.

- Wonneberger, Astrid. *Salvaging the Past – Shaping the Future. Perceptions of Changes in the South Docklands*. Dietrich Reimer Verlag GmbH, 2009.

Housing in troubled times: Spitalfields, St. James's Walk, McCaffrey's and Fairbrother's Fields Housing

Catherine Scuffil, Historian in Residence, Dublin South Central

Following the collapse of tenements in Dublin's Church Street in 1913 with fatal consequences, pressure grew on authorities to address the chronic housing conditions that existed in Dublin at the time. The provision of new and refurbished housing was almost halted by the beginning of the First World War despite a £4 million offer from the British Treasury towards housing which, it was considered, would serve to 'encourage conscription' in Dublin. The failure of this offer to materialise was exacerbated by the need to rebuild the destroyed city centre following the 1916 Rising.

Despite this turbulent time in Irish history, Dublin Corporation established a Housing Committee for the provision of new, well-designed housing for low-income citizens. The committee chairman was Alderman Thomas (Tom) Kelly, a popular Sinn Féin councillor who had been imprisoned following the Rising. The committee members also included Alfie Byrne, later Lord Mayor of Dublin, and W.T. Cosgrave, a 1916 Rising veteran and future President of the Executive Council of the Irish Free State.

A survey carried out by this committee in early 1918 showed a worsening housing situation in Dublin. Almost 90,000 (29 per cent) of the population lived in slums considered unfit for human habitation with 20,000 families living in one-roomed tenements. The conditions created breeding grounds for the spread of illnesses and disease, with consequent high mortality rates especially among the young. This survey set the scene for the Housing Committee to commence building a series of small social housing developments despite the ongoing events of the First World War.

Alderman Kelly immediately identified that 'significant developments' could be carried out on the southside of the city at Spitalfields – between Francis Street and Meath Street in the city's Liberties, and also in Fairbrother's Fields, between Cork Street and Dublin's South Circular Road. These sites were already in Corporation ownership. Finding it difficult to obtain funding, he proposed applying for an 'American Loan' in order to proceed with house building on the above, together with McCaffrey Estate in the Mount Brown/Kilmainham area and at St. James's Walk beside the Grand Canal Main Line near Guinness's Brewery. Alderman Kelly may not have intended to follow through with the American loan, but the threat at least worked, with the British Treasury eventually agreeing to provide financial assistance for house building in Dublin city.

Of the four areas mentioned for development, St. James's Walk and Fairbrother's Fields were open fields and McCaffrey's was an orchard in the South Dublin Union, the large workhouse and hospital on the edge of the city. Spitalfields was the only site requiring 'clear and build' – the demolition of existing poor-quality tenement and ruined buildings that were considered beyond repair.

In former times Spitalfields was a busy, prosperous area. Rocque's map of Dublin (1756) shows nearby Francis Street and Carman's Hall as a populous area in the heart of the then fashionable city. Street directories of the time list successful merchants, manufacturers and traders. Indeed, Jonathan Swift's book *Drapier's Letters* (a play on the word 'Draper') were all addressed, 'from my shop in St. Francis Street.' The many retail houses were frequented daily by the nobility.

Trades in Spitalfields included boot, brogue and clay-pipe making; shops selling tobacco and snuff; wigs and curled hair; tabinet (fine quality silk and worsted fabric), silk and poplin weaving; and hosiery and velvet making – all of which served the needs of a fashion-conscious nobility. Older industries such as nail-making, soap-boiling, brewing and whip-making were also represented. The nearby streets, lanes and alleys had large factories dealing in bran, butter, groceries and general provisions. The adjacent street called the Coombe was a more industrialised area, with weavers, silk-dyers, a brush factory, pump-makers and a large iron-monger and merchant called John Parkes based there. In general, every premises along the Coombe was occupied by either a drapers, haberdashers or tailor. Francis Street itself showed evidence of industrial activity on all sides.

But by 1840, the whole area was in decline. Sir John Gilbert's 1840 *Quarterly Review* commented that Dublin, the nation's capital, was formerly the home of the Irish National Seat of Legislature that created a centre of intellectual and industrial activity. This all changed with the passing of the Irish Act of Union in 1800 and the consequent removal of the Irish Parliament the following year, meaning Irish MPs had to go to Westminster in London instead of attending the Irish Parliament on College Green. All of this was a heavy blow for Dublin. Each subsequent decade saw the decline of local manufacturing industries. Forty years later, Dublin was nothing but a distribution warehouse for products from abroad with a working population almost totally dependent on casual labour. A huge number of Dubliners had a meagre existence and lived in poor-quality housing or rooms.

Some social housing building had taken place in the Coombe area during the late 1800s, most notably by the Dublin Artisans' Dwellings Company (DADC), a semi-philanthropic private enterprise aiming to provide quality housing for Dublin's working classes. The Iveagh Trust (founded in 1890 by Edward Guinness and initially a part of the Guinness Trust) had also built apartments in Patrick Street, which included community facilities such as public swimming baths, a wash-house and hostel.

In 1909 Alderman Kelly used John Gilbert's review as a template to examine the prosperity or otherwise of the Liberties of Dublin. This made for sobering reading:

> *Going through these streets and alleys today, as I have constantly done, there is little or no evidence to the eye that there are any of the industries left.*

> *Messrs. Taylor's tobacco factory is still in Francis Street, and Messrs. Parkes' large distributing establishment is still in the Coombe, but I can find no evidence of the other manufacturers mentioned.*

> *I looked through last year's Directory to see what it had to tell, and this is what I found: In Francis Street sixty of the houses are marked "tenements" and fourteen "ruins"; Mark's Alley, mainly "tenements"; Swift's Alley, "tenements"; Ashe Street, all "tenements." In Garden lane and Spitalfields there are a couple of bacon factors mentioned, and the rest seem to be "tenements."*

In April 1917 the *Evening Herald* announced that £100,000 had been made available by the British Treasury for the four identified developments. It also carried an additional comment, 'the only scheme of the four that there is a particular objection to by a large section of the public is Spitalfields Scheme in the Francis Street district.' It added that the scheme, 'embraces a lot of slum property' and that 'it would clear the air of suspicion if the public were told who owned the properties.' In addition, the ratepayers' bill for the final developments would be in the region of £52,000. It later transpired that some councillors on the corporation were the owners of the properties in question.

Later that month, the *Freeman's Journal* reported on a City Hall enquiry being held into the development at Spitalfields. Two early attendees at this enquiry were Reverend McCreery, rector of St. Werburg's and Fr. McSweeney of Meath Street parish. Both were, 'in favour of the site and considered very sanitary dwellings could be erected there.' Later, Reverend Fr. Monahan of St. Nicholas of Myra parish, Francis Street stated that, 'houses are needed. The scheme has the approval of employers and employees in the neighbourhood.' Responding, the enquiry inspector said that the, 'remarkable thing is that so few Dublin employers have built houses for workers, the only exception I can think of is Guinness.'

At a meeting of the Dublin Tenants' Association in July 1917 Denis Larkin (brother of trade-unionist James) stated that 'Spitalfields will add £1,600 to the annual deficit with only 75 three roomed houses built for 369 people, most of whom will have been evicted off the site in the first place.'

When the development at Spitalfields finally went ahead, the Corporation established the rent for each new three roomed 'cottage' – the term used for all housing types - at a subsidised 5s 6d per week. A city council meeting confirmed that the 'real' rent was considerably higher at 13s 6d, representing an overall loss to Dublin Corporation of over £13,000 per annum.

Sir John Griffith, civil engineer and politician, considered that the proposed density on the site was too great, and that every effort should be made to provide gardens for individual houses. This was not followed through at Spitalfields, however, a small shared public recreation square was provided at Park Terrace instead.

The *Freeman's Journal* of 28 April 1918 announced that the tender to proceed with the development of the first phase of houses in the Spitalfields area was accepted. Work would commence with the total demolition of all existing properties followed

by the erection of 75 new properties in the area. The successful bidders were Messrs
J. and M. Clarke, Upper Clanbrassil Street who had a builder's yard at Wellington
Place near Harold's Cross bridge.

The total cost of the tender was £22,918, higher than expected. Despite this, Dublin
Corporation agreed to provide an extra £405 in order to install one electric light in
each newly constructed house.

Spitalfields, looking towards Meath Street, 1960s
(courtesy of Dublin City Library and Archives)

The Spitalfields scheme was dogged with uncertainty. By July 1918, Dublin Corporation's
debt associated with the scheme was £30,000, with more money urgently needed
to prevent a complete close-down of the build. It was proving difficult to get local
finance, 'People who made money in the city and the banks particularly in every
instance refused to give the Committee any financial assistance.' The continuing
First World War was creating shortages, with regular problems in obtaining building
materials. This had an unexpected advantage for Irish suppliers, with locally sourced
wood and bricks used in construction.

The houses finally opened in 1918, with the original street names retained in Park
Terrace, Carman's Hall, Catherine Street (related to the local parish), Ash Street and
Spitalfields itself.

Park Terrace, The Coombe, 1977 (courtesy of Dublin City Library and Archives)

The *Thomas Street and Environs, Architectural Conservation Area* (2009) document noted that the architecture of the Spitalfields local authority housing was closely modelled on and a 'single most accomplished example' of the earlier housing developments of the DADC, adding that, 'the design of the scheme is influenced by the concept of the picturesque Garden Suburb, with gridded paired and Wyatt sash windows, brick and pebbledash treatment to facades, and polychromatic brickwork to chimneys and gables.'

While the Spitalfields houses were under construction, work also commenced on a mixed scheme of single and two storey cottages on a raised site on the then towing path of the Grand Canal Main Line. This site was bounded on the southern side by a laneway known as St. James's Walk or the Back of the Pipes, where a watercourse of the river Poddle ran in both an open channel and partial culvert near a house called Mountainview. The name, St. James's Walk would later transfer to the new road created on the towing path. The site was considered suitable for houses, due to its proximity to large employers such as Guinness, the distillery at Marrowbone Lane and the Grand Canal headquarters.

The area was midway between the city's Liberties and the urban village of Dolphin's Barn, where the local brickworks, another significant local employer, was located. Dolphin's Barn bricks would be used in the construction.

When completed the scheme provided accommodation for 66 families arranged
around four different terraces. In an acknowledgement to the comments of Sir John
Griffith during the development of Spitalfields, some houses at St. James's Walk facing
the Grand Canal had small front gardens, together with a shared kitchen garden for
the entire estate on the west side of the scheme.

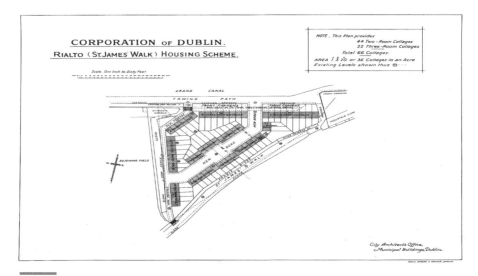

Plans for St. James's Walk Housing Scheme
(courtesy of Dublin City Library and Archives)

The early drawings for St. James's Walk indicated nameless 'new roads' in the
development. Perhaps reflecting the heightened Irish political situation following
the end of the First World War, Dublin Corporation subsequently agreed to a 1916
tribute-naming scheme for the completed development, resulting in Clarke's Terrace
(Thomas Clarke), Colbert's Fort (Con Colbert), Mallin Avenue (Michael Mallin), all of
whom had been executed for their part in the 1916 Rising, and McCarthy Terrace for
Captain Tom McCarthy, the Commanding Officer in Marrowbone Lane Distillery, an
outpost during the 1916 Rising.

When it came to designing the houses and layout of McCaffrey Estate, Mount Brown,
in 1919, Dublin Corporation called upon the assistance of Thomas Joseph (TJ) Byrne, an
architect with radical views on raising standards for social housing. One key feature
of Byrne's houses was a parlour as an individual retreat from the rest of the house, a
feature that was to continue for most housing developments in the future Irish Free
State government. Byrne also preferred to include an indoor toilet and bathroom.

Colbert's Fort, St. James's Walk, 1975 (courtesy of Dublin City Library and Archives)

Large gardens were provided, where possible, to enable the future residents to grow their own fruit and vegetables.

The proposal to erect houses on the McCaffrey estate was first considered by the Corporation in 1914. At that time, it was proposed to erect 240 houses. Concerns were raised about the uninspired and monotonous layout in the plans, described as, 'narrow straight laneways, monotonous rows of red brick dwellings, enforced absence of foliage, and backyards of a few square feet abutting on each other.' These comments were instrumental in bringing Byrne in as a consultant, as he had 'a great deal of experience in the erection of working class dwellings.'

Byrne took on the McCaffrey estate project as a private commission, at a discounted fee of 1 per cent of the overall cost of the build (the going rate was 5 per cent). He designed a scheme at a lower density to the original, with a completely different layout. The Corporation's Housing Committee approved his plans in 1915, but due to difficulties presented by the First World War, the loan was refused by the Local Government Board (LGB).

In 1917 Dublin Corporation reapplied to the LGB for a building loan for McCaffrey Estate. The amount requested was increased, as costs had risen in the two years. Byrne submitted additional improvements to the overall scheme in October 1917 prior

to tenders being sought in January 1918. Mr Louis Monks, builder, from Kingstown
(Dun Laoghaire) was the successful bidder, with a tender for £76,800. In 1919, work
eventually commenced on the construction of 202 houses on the site.

By August 1919, only 80 houses had been built, and some 2,000 applicants for the
homes had been received. Completion was affected by industrial action and ongoing
funding difficulties, as well as domestic issues related to the War of Independence.
As work continued, W.T. Cosgrave developed an appreciation of the skills of Byrne.
This was evident at a city council meeting in July 1921 when Cosgrave defended
Byrne by emphasising the progress made despite all the difficulties endured during
construction, insisting that, 'only for Mr. Byrne, there would not have been a brick
laid on the McCaffrey Estate now, or possibly for years to come.'

Like St. James's Walk, the early plans for McCaffrey Estate did not include names for the
roads. Dublin Corporation again agreed a 1916 tribute-naming scheme, immediately
re-naming the entire estate Ceannt Fort, (for Commandant Éamonn Ceannt) with
individual roads being called after volunteers who had been killed in the South Dublin
Union during the Rising. Included was Burke Place, named after Frank 'Goban' Burke,
step-brother of W.T. Cosgrave who had been killed on the second day of the Rising.

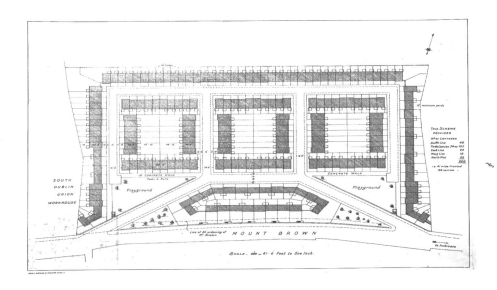

Plans for McCaffrey Estate Housing Scheme
(courtesy of Dublin City Library and Archives)

McCaffrey Estate
(courtesy of Dublin City
Library and Archives)

The completed Ceannt Fort estate has been described as, 'a wonderfully intimate series of housing clusters, gardens and playgrounds, and is regarded as one of the finest examples of urban housing of its day.'

The final and largest estate to be built at this time was the Fairbrother's Fields development between Cork Street and the South Circular Road which eventually provided over 430 houses for the citizens of Dublin. As well as the main field, a small number of properties around the Ardee Street boundary were compulsorily purchased and cleared by the Corporation and added to extend the site. This area had long associations with Huguenot weavers of the 17th century, reflected in the nearby Tenter Lane, an old access route across the site leading to the old tenterhook fields, where the weavers had stretched out their cloth to dry.

As the Dublin Corporation workforce was rebuilding the city centre following the turbulent times of the revolutionary years, the scheme at Fairbrother's Fields was also put out to tender. The intention was to use a number of different building contractors to work on the entire project, each assigned a different section to complete. Among these were the Dublin Building Guild, the Municipal Workshops and a private company, J.L. Wilde & Co, Ltd. This resulted in a mixed development of housing styles, each complimenting the other, all with front and back gardens. There was also reserved space for a future school, a public park and plans to construct a new Roman Catholic Church.

As efforts continued to assist local employment during the early years of the Free State, construction companies were encouraged to buy locally produced products for any works undertaken. The nearby Dolphin's Barn Brick Company again provided bricks for the construction of 357 houses at the Fairbrother's Fields in 1922.

Oscar Square, Fairbrother's Fields, 1996
(courtesy of Dublin City Library and Archives)

Alderman Kelly was responsible for the naming of the roads in the completed scheme. Whilst, as we have seen, the initial developments incorporated street names related to revolutionary figures with associations to the 1916 Rising, those built in the initial years of Irish independence included names associated with the Celtic Revival. Roads were called after James Clarence Mangan, George Petrie, John O'Donovan, Eugene O'Curry and Jeremiah O'Leary to name but a few – tributes to historians and poets, with a nod to Saint Thomas's Abbey and to Irish legend and folklore in Oscar Square – commemorating Oscar the son of Oisín. Kelly's overall intention of housing the people of Dublin and educating the youth is reflected in choosing the names as he did. This was surely his most enduring legacy. Today, the original Fairbrother's Fields scheme, and other adjacent houses, are collectively known as 'The Tenters', a direct link-back to the original use of the land in the area.

Spitalfields scheme houses at Carman's Hall, showing date 1918 in gable (courtesy of John Buckley)

(opposite)
St. James's Walk scheme, houses at Colbert's Fort

(right)
McCaffrey Estate, Owens Avenue

(bottom)
Fairbrother's Fields houses at St Thomas's Road showing date 1922 in gable

(All courtesy of John Buckley)

The building of these four estates was a most remarkable achievement, especially considering the cascade of international and national events that played out in the background as construction was being planned and when it was underway. In the evolving eras of the First World War, the Easter Rising, the War of Independence, the subsequent Civil War and eventually the formation of the Irish Free State, quality, modern housing with the latest facilities of the time was achieved within an approximate two-mile square area.

Houses in all four estates are very desirable and much sought after homes today. They have proved relatively easy to modernise, modify and also to extend as family homes over the past 100 years. Some existing residents are direct descendants of the original home-owners, and this has created a strong sense of community and supportive neighbourhoods. It is true to say that the estates have stood the test of time and represent a true legacy of Alderman Tom Kelly and Dublin Corporation's Housing Committee operating at a time of great uncertainty, difficulty and change.

Further Reading

- Original housing development plans 1914–1922, Dublin City Library and Archive. *With special thanks to Mary Clark, Dublin City Archivist*

- Minutes of Dublin Corporation 1913-1923, Dublin City Library and Archive

- Thoms Directories, Dublin City Library and Archive

- Personal communication Maria O'Reilly, Tenters Residents Association

- CASEY, CHRISTINE. *The Buildings of Ireland – Dublin.* Yale University Press, 2005.

- CIVIC TRUST. *Thomas Street and Environs, Architectural Conservation Area,* adopted by Dublin City Council 07/09/2009

- DALY, MARY E. *Dublin the Deposed Capital, A Social and Economic History 1860–1914.* Cork University Press, 1984.

- SCUFFIL, CATHERINE (ED.). Dolphin's Barn Historical Society *By the Sign of the Dolphin, the Story of Dolphin's Barn.* Elo Press, 1993.

- FEWER, MICHAEL & JOHN BYRNE. *TJ Byrne, Nation Builder.* South Dublin Libraries, 2013.

- McMANUS RUTH. *Dublin 1910–1940.* Four Courts Press, 2002.

- YEATES, PÁDRAIG. *A City in Turmoil Dublin, 1919–1921.* Gill & Macmillan, 2012.

Suggested reading: Dublin Memoirs do you remember...

'When I die, Dublin will be written on my heart' is a famous quote from a famous Dubliner, James Joyce. Dublin is a city that has shaped the lives of all those who have called it home, whether that's been for a few months or all their lives. There have been some excellent memoirs written about life in Dublin and here are some reading suggestions from the Historians in Residence:

MAEVE CASSERLY
The Springs of Affection
by Maeve Brennan

While it's not technically a memoir, these short stories by the famous writer for *Harper's Bazaar* and *The New Yorker*, beautifully capture her childhood growing up in Ranelagh in the oftentimes chaotic home of her revolutionary parents, Úna and Robert Brennan. Although Maeve left Ireland for the US in her teens, most of her work is based around the world of middle-class, suburban Dublin.

JAMES CURRY
The Boy on the Back Wall & Other Essays
by James Plunkett

A personal and charming collection of essays, written between 1961 and 1986, which reflect the lifelong interests and concerns of an author who deserves to be remembered for more than his landmark historical novel *Strumpet City* (1969). Among the most memorable sections of the book are Plunkett's loving recollections of his Dublin childhood, vivid memories of labour leader Jim Larkin, and 'potted biographies' of the likes of Seán O'Casey, Frank O'Connor, Peadar O'Donnell and Oliver St John Gogarty.

BERNARD KELLY
Mr Smyllie, Sir
by Tony Gray

This book provides an insight into the chaotic and idiosyncratic world of R.M. Smyllie, the legendary editor of the *Irish Times* between 1934 and 1954.

CORMAC MOORE
Dublin Made Me
by Todd Andrews

Dublin Made Me is a riveting first-hand account of Todd Andrew's youth that was shaped by his involvement in extraordinary times, through his participation in the Easter Rising, War of Independence and Civil War.

MARY MULDOWNEY
44 A Dublin Memoir
by Peter Sheridan

A wonderful memoir about growing up in the 1960s in Dublin. While the focus of the book is primarily on the Sheridan family and their relationships with each other, their lodgers and their neighbours, it is also a celebration of living in a working-class area of Dublin. It does not avoid the harsher realities of life in Ireland at that time but is nevertheless a funny, bitter-sweet love letter to Sheridan's (and my) beloved city.

CATHERINE SCUFFIL
Me Jewel and Darlin' Dublin
by Éamonn MacThomáis

Full of stories of Dublin City, and the people who live there told from the heart, with historical events and facts worked into the story. A lovely social history.